Deep Dive

Existential Essays for Personal Transformation

by
Dan Beeman

Published by Intrepid Souls Press

www.danbman.com

ISBN: 9798673612828

"When we are motivated by goals that have deep meaning, by dreams that need completion, by pure love that needs expressing, then we truly live life."
— Greg Anderson

This book is for all people who want to look beyond news, dive deeper into issues, and spend time to reflect internally. It is an exploration into topics such as Success. Happiness. Passion. Purpose. Sustainability. Faith. Religion. Politics. Culture. Power. Freedom. God. Hypocrisy. Parenting. Family. Fear. Trust. Love. Work. Social Media/Technology.

It is in honor of those who came before us. It is *for* those who come after us.

It is dedicated to our children.

The Dive Map

5

FOREWORD
—SIMONA KSOLL

I just can't get myself to get started… is something that I often hear as a coach.

The truth is that everything starts with a decision.

When an idea takes shape on the screen of our mind it's just that, an idea.

Unless we decide to act on it, that's all it's ever going to be.

The reason why so many people don't get started on a great idea is because they worry too much about what other people are going to say or think about them if they do.

That's how entire visions never get realized.

That's how infinite potential remains dormant and million-dollar ideas go back to the Universal drawing board to be picked up by somebody else.

I have a friend who a few years back had the phenomenal idea of creating jackets out of vintage kimonos.

That's all she talked about but she never took a single step in the direction of making it happen, until one day these stylish jackets appeared at Bloomingdales.

Somebody else received the same idea from the Universe, ran with it, and made a fortune.

There are those who can't bring themselves to get started and those who get it done.

Dan Beeman, the author of this book, is a guy that gets it done.

Be it in his career as an executive in the hospitality industry maximizing revenue opportunities, writing a movie script and fearlessly pitching it to Hollywood executives, championing pickleball as its ambassador to Mexico, or writing this book, the minute the idea forms in his mind, he's taking action to make it happen.

I met Dan while he was writing this book. He had rented a beach-front property on the Mexican Riviera for a month at the beginning of the California lock-down and committed himself to writing and curating essays from fellow contributors on a wide variety of existentialist topics.

The intention of this book is to dive deeper into issues beyond the news media and reflect on them internally as we collectively navigate these uncertain times, united as mankind on Earth.

The essays in this book explore questions like:

Why are we here?

What is our collective purpose?

What is the individual's purpose?

How does what we do impact our world?

At the end of the month, inspired by his daily beach walks and swimming in the healing waters of the Caribbean, Dan, a self-proclaimed lover of all things aquatic and a dive enthusiast, wrote most of the book you're about to dive into.

Everything starts with a decision, then it's about getting it done.

This is how we contribute to the whole and increase our impact and influence in the world.

The ripple effects of taking an idea and turning it into a reality, in this case the book that you see before you, are profound.

Simona Ksoll
Business Strategist & Personal Mentor

Deep Dive

ABOUT THE TITLE
—DAN BEEMAN

The "Deep Dive" title is a metaphor for the work we will do together—taking a deep dive within ourselves—and was chosen in part because I am a lover of almost everything aquatic, like swimming in the ocean, body surfing, floating, free-diving, snorkeling, and scuba diving.

I learned to swim just months after I learned how to walk. I've had some of the most powerful experiences of my life in the water.

As a teenager, I created a self-soothing meditational exercise for myself that I call bouncing. I would be in about 10 feet of water and bounce up and down from the bottom of the pool to the surface for 30 minutes to an hour, while modulating my breath and humming with bubbles while exhaling. It was deeply relaxing.

Another peak aquatic experience was swimming with a dolphin named JoJo in Turks and Caicos Island 25-30 times over a six-month period. He was a wild dolphin estranged from his pod. He was playful and fun. I would follow him, and he would let me get close but never touch him.

The other was and is Watsu and Water Dancing. It is one of the most powerful experiences you can have in the water. It is a moving journey into your subconscious—almost going back to a womb-like experience.

The deeply relaxing effects of warm water and the nurturing support of the Watsu giver, combined with movements, stretches, massage, and pressure-point work, create a range of therapeutic benefits and potential healing on many levels for the Watsu receiver.

Inika Spence, Healing Dance. Photo by Marilyn Brownell.

Back into the womb...nothing to accomplish, just be.

*Imagine, the warmth and sense of weightlessness induced by water...
your eyes closed, so there is just the play of light across your eyelids;
your ears are under the water so the sound of the world is muffled.*

*The world starts to disappear, leaving just yourself and your
experience of your body and being in the water, nothing to do,
nowhere to go, just receiving and letting go, into the graceful
movement, rocking, cradling, and gentle rhythm.*

It is no wonder people speak of states of bliss and levels of
relaxation never before imagined.

Over time, with experience in Watsu, I was also lucky enough
to experience something deeper called Healing Dance with
Inika Spence. First, the receiver is gently floated and moved
through a series of stretches to warm up the body and reach
full relaxation.

The giver guides the receiver into a state of deep relaxation as
preparation to go under the water.

A powerful aspect of Healing Dance is the attention to the
breath.

It becomes the giver's complete focus to tune in with the
receiver, and support and encourage the receiver to relax into a
deeper awareness of their being, body, and breath.

A profound level of trust and surrender then becomes the key
to safe passage through the doorway between the two worlds

Inika Spence, Healing Dance. Photo by Marilyn Brownell.

above and below the water's surface.

When the giver feels that the client is relaxed and ready, the underwater journey can begin.

After a full inhalation, the receiver's face is then slowly turned toward the surface of the water and gently allowed to submerge.

Gradually the giver can take the receiver for longer periods under water, moving them through a dance of movements. This sense of freedom is an ideal state to release any holding patterns, whether physical, mental, or emotional, and open to reconnecting with the joy of one's essential nature and what many describe as "coming home."

A natural phenomenon known as the "diving reflex" begins to take effect as the water brushes across the receiver's face. This causes the heart rate, blood pressure, and metabolism to slow

16   *Deep Dive*

down, contributing to the ability to stay effortlessly under the water. When the receiver is ready to re-emerge, a natural cue is transmitted and s/he is brought up to the surface. Inhalation is once again triggered by the feeling of air on the face. Plenty of time is provided between submerging and re-oxygenating breathing.

My other aquatic "accomplishments" have included becoming a certified scuba instructor, diving to 321 feet, swimming eight miles across Lake Geneva, WI, swimming from San Francisco around Alcatraz and back without a wet suit, winning the Aquatic Distance Challenge 10K swim for my age group in Santa Monica, and creating open water challenges in Panama and Belize.

All that, but I never learned how to, and still can't float!

*Thanks to www.natural-health-zone.com/healing-power-of-water.html for some of the information in this essay.

Dan Beeman, competing in the Alcatraz triathlon

Deep Dive

INTRODUCTION
—DAN BEEMAN

This book is a collection of essays on topics concerning the existence of mankind on Earth. Essay authors have been chosen to write personal essays on areas of their expertise or interest.

How did we get here?

Why are we here?

What are we doing here?

Where are we going from here?

These are the existential questions we will explore. They all have to do with our existence on Earth.

Will we definitively answer these questions for you?

No. That's impossible—for many reasons.
But we will try to help you answer them for yourself.

How we got here, why we are here, and where we are going from here, is merely conjecture.

Atheists (those who do not believe in God) will say that our being here is merely the confluence of chance, matter, and time.

Theists (those who believe in God) believe that we are human manifestations in the image of God, the creator of all things.

Their differences of opinion are a matter of debate for another forum, so we will leave those questions for scientists, philosophers, and religious scholars.

We will focus on what we are doing here, because that is the most answerable by using provable, factual data.

We have a pretty good idea of what we are doing here, because our collective human actions have historical imprints and attendant consequences. Those actions, over time, also result in verifiable change to humankind, the planet, and all living things on Earth.

Those changes are often referred to as evolution. But, contrary to popular belief, human evolution is not on a vertical line of continual improvement, since there are periods of growth and decline over millions of years.

While scientific evolution is incremental (built upon previous knowledge), human evolution is not, because the human experience is an ongoing experiment. The image below is sarcastic but illustrates the direction of evolution since the advent of the agricultural age.

Maybe the better question is: Why are we doing what we are doing here?

Another way to phrase that is asking the question: What is our collective purpose?

Then, diving deeper, we occasionally ask ourselves about our individual purpose.

Our book is, therefore, a Self-Socratic Endeavor—an exploration of ourselves by questioning the choices we make in our lives.

A byproduct of "What is mankind doing and why?" is "What are the impacts of what we are doing here on Earth?"

We will be discussing both—our individual purpose and impact. Then, we will dive deeper to understand collective, societal purpose and impact.

These questions led to the idea for this book, which I am writing for my kids and their kids.

Never stop exploring.

Always be curious.

Seek adventure.

Work together.

The essays in this book will discuss the issues and components of human nature, behavior, relationships, emotions, motivations, and contexts.

While we will explore these endeavors as objectively as possible, we also acknowledge our limitations, and that my point of view comes from the first-world perspective of an educated, western male.

We want this book to flow like a metaphor of scuba diving at night.

Deep Dive will be our metaphysical and quasi-aquatic journey together.

First, as with a safety briefing on a boat before the dive, I will introduce myself in this section and in "About Me."

Then, I will outline the plan for the dive—what we can expect to see, the obstacles that inhibit our vision, and limitations to seeing it all clearly in "Existentialism" and "Distractions."

Then, we will enter the water and descend. We will follow my flashlight to make new discoveries together. And you will use your flashlight to see things that I may have missed or discover them on your own in the essays of "Part 2: The Self," "Part 3: Society/Humankind," "Part 4: God / Religion," and "Part 5: Earth."

Near the end of the dive, we will settle on the bottom, turn our lights off, and just breathe, think, and be in "Summary."

Then, we will ascend together. When we reach the surface, the water will wash from our masks. We will be coming from a place of dynamic exploration, new discoveries, deep peace, and a sense of knowing ourselves—and be in awe of the human experience, nature, and the entire galaxy as it opens itself up to our eyes like the first time we saw it.

Refreshed. Rejuvenated. Reinvented.

Flying Iguana Asana on a homemade waterslide

INSPIRATION

Before we define Existentialism, it is important to shine light on the inspirational material that helped me on my personal journey.

I read and re-read the following books many times. As Covey says, "sharpen the saw" to keep the mind and good ideas fresh.

While none of them are specifically about Existentialism, they are all about the human experience. And Existentialism is all about the human experience.

The Four Agreements: A Practical Guide to Personal Freedom

Be impeccable with your word—Tell the truth.

Don't take anything personally—Be subject-oriented. Know and love the self.

Don't assume. You know what happens. It leads to gossip. Gossip is for weak minds. Strive to speak of ideas rather than of specific people, and never speak in a derogatory manner.

Always do your best—Your best is not necessarily perfect, which is okay.

OR

The Seven Spiritual Laws of Success—A Practical Guide to the Fulfillment of Your Dreams is freely inspired by Hinduist and spiritualistic concepts, which preach the idea that personal success is not the outcome of hard work, precise plans, or a driving ambition, but rather of understanding our basic nature as human beings and how to follow the laws of nature.

OR

Ishmael is a 1992 philosophical novel by Daniel Quinn. The novel examines the hidden cultural biases driving modern civilization and explores themes of ethics, sustainability, and global catastrophe. Largely framed as a Socratic conversation between two characters, *Ishmael* aims to expose several widely accepted assumptions of modern society, such as human supremacy and other cultural myths that produce catastrophic consequences for humankind and the environment.

OR

The 7 Habits of Highly Effective People, in which Franklin Covey presents an approach to being effective in attaining goals by aligning oneself to what he calls "true north" principles based on a character ethic that he presents as universal and timeless.

We will be exploring lots of the teachings of these authors in the following pages. Specifically, Covey's material, because he advocates purpose and a purpose-driven life.

This is the "why" to the "what" of our presence on Earth.

He talks a lot about perception, perception bias, and the difference between character-driven and personality-driven behaviors. These are the fascinating subjects and insights that we will explore.

OR

In his 1946 book, *Man's Search for Meaning*, Viktor Frankl chronicled his experiences as a prisoner in Nazi concentration camps during World War II. His writing involved identifying a purpose in life to feel positive about, and then imagining that outcome.

OR

No Excuses: Existentialism and the Meaning of Life Audio CD—January 1, 2000, by Robert C. Solomon.

"What is life? What is my place in it? What choices do these questions obligate me to make?" More than a half-century after it burst upon the intellectual scene—with roots that extend to the mid-19th century—existentialism's quest to answer these most fundamental questions of individual responsibility, morality, and personal freedom has continued to exert a profound attraction.

"Existentialism is, in my view, the most exciting and important philosophical movement of the past century and a half," says Professor Solomon. "Fifty years after the French philosopher Jean-Paul Sartre gave it its identity, and 150 years after the Danish philosopher Søren Kierkegaard gave it its initial impetus, it continues to win new enthusiasts."

OR

Sapiens: A Brief History of Humankind is a book by Yuval Noah Harari, first published in Hebrew in Israel in 2011, based on a series of lectures Harari taught at The Hebrew University of Jerusalem, and in English in 2014. The book surveys the history of humankind from the evolution of archaic human species in the Stone Age up to the twenty-first century, focusing on Homo sapiens. The account is situated within a framework provided by the natural sciences, particularly evolutionary biology.

OR

The Alchemist is subtitled "A Fable About Following Your Dreams." The universal point this story makes is that everyone has a special destiny, and yet not everyone resolves to attain it because it takes hard work. Reaching one's destiny requires leaving behind familiar surroundings. It also demands persistence, the ability to change when appropriate, and the willingness to respond to omens that point the way. The constant theme in *The Alchemist* is to pursue your dreams by following what your heart desires. During the young boy's journey, he learns to listen to his heart and follow the language of omens. With each passing obstacle and hurdle that the young boy encounters, there is a lesson to learn.

ABOUT ME
—DAN BEEMAN

In order to engage you, the reader, in this process, I'd like to share more about myself, in the form of two biographies.

The first is a professional biography that comes from the vantage point of my professional persona, including stories of my success.

The other is a personal biography that comes from honest introspection with details about some inspirations. I am doing this so you can learn about me as the author of this book. And, as an example, because I am going to ask you to write both kinds of biographies as your first exercise in understanding yourself better. They will be helpful to you as a baseline to build upon other work we will be doing later in the book.

Dan Beeman

Summary—From jumping out of perfectly good aircraft as a U.S. Army, Airborne Paratrooper in Germany, to diving more than 300 feet as a deep-water SCUBA Instructor in the Caribbean, Dan Beeman has shown remarkable range in his life pursuits.

At the tender age of 50, he went back to graduate school and earned his Master of Hospitality from UNLV, where he studied Tourism with a specialization in Sustainable Tourism. He wrote his final research paper on "The Implications of Pickleball for the Hospitality Industry."

The conclusions of the research: Resorts and clubs that have either tennis or basketball courts that do not add pickleball are not maximizing potential revenue or their asset value. They are also losing market share, group travel, and growth opportunities.

Beeman seized upon this knowledge and his background in driving new revenue through creative sponsorships, partnerships, and events. He launched his consulting practice to help his clients succeed.

He has also recently written a screenplay for a buddy comedy about two former tennis champions who

Our dinner table was filled with chaos (seven kids), information, and dynamic conversation. Our father would sit at the head of the table and interrogate all of us about our day. He would ask what we learned, what we saw, who we met, and what we did. We were blessed to be led by a man who was a slow eater and naturally curious about each one of us. Our television exposure was mostly limited to Sunday night viewing of *60 Minutes* and the *Andy Williams Show.*

My parents were, and are, big proponents of Catholicism. We all received a Jesuit education at some point. However, humanism permeated our life experience. We were taught and it was often reinforced that we can do and be whoever or whatever we want in life, if we are willing to do the work. That faith gave us all confidence to pursue our individual destinies and led to great success.

My dad and I still talk on the phone frequently. He challenges me to invert the concept of "How is life treating me?" to "How am I treating my life?"

I walked to and from school every day with our neighbors through the 8th grade. After school, we would play in the yard or at the park until the dinner bell rang.

Yes, we had a dinner bell!

Our outdoor activities were not very structured (compared with those of kids today), and that led to a lot of creative game playing. I attribute any of my creative skills to a combination of the DNA from my parents and the experiences of my childhood—not watching television and playing freely with friends. We didn't have cell phones or social media.

Oh, the joy of innocence and a simple existence!

In high school, I discovered and indulged in frequent marijuana use. It led to passivity, lethargy, and apathy about school. I was also very immature and entitled. I had no sense of direction or purpose. It is no wonder my parents opted to emancipate me from their domain (i.e., booted me out) days after I turned 18. I was a bad influence on my younger brother, five years my junior. I definitely "earned" the right to figure it out on my own, without anyone to protect me.

I have been exploring ever since.

My next decision had a huge impact on the trajectory of my life. One day, I went from a being a child, and acting like one, to having responsibilities for myself.

I enlisted in the U.S. Army.

It was a huge wake-up call.

It scared the hell out of my parents.

It was also an existential epiphany: I discovered that I needed to take charge of my life.

But before I could, I needed to get my ass kicked around a bit.

And boy, did I ever!

In basic training, I learned that no preferences would be given to me. I couldn't talk my way out of situations, and I was held accountable for all my actions.

I learned that nobody cared about my opinion. I was a number, not a name. I had no freedom. My long hair was buzzed to the scalp. The parties were over. I learned that I could trust no one.

I learned things like meritocracy, to appreciate diversity, and that each person is a unique individual. I learned that racism is stupid, to make my bed, to work hard, persevere, manifest destiny, watch my back, and take advantage of opportunities.

I learned that nobody owes you anything.

I have some great memories and some recurring nightmares. I lived with and learned from people of different ethnicities.

In the trenches, race, orientation, and religion are irrelevant. Working together is paramount.

Real, sustainable success requires teamwork.

I learned that whatever I wanted and whoever I wanted to be was up to me.

I had to create my own destiny.

I earned an invitation after basic training to become an airborne paratrooper. This was another incredible experience for me, as I was able to overcome a fear of heights and jump out of airplanes. Next, they offered me the opportunity to go to Ranger School. I declined.

After airborne school, I was stationed at the 3rd Armored Division in Germany, where I served for 18 months. During this time, I was also fortunate enough to be included on the 3rd Armored Division swim team. We traveled and competed in swim meets and experienced the culture and the beauty of different areas of Germany. This was during the Cold War, and the United States employed Pershing missiles in West Germany to protect our western European allies against East Germany and the Soviet Union.

While in Germany, I often read about and explored my inner conflict of serving as a peacekeeper, yet, at the same time, an agent of war. I learned that I'm a pacifist by nature and I hate guns because I have experienced people doing very stupid things with them.

In the end, I served two years and was discharged honorably.

Looking back on that time, I learned many things, but most importantly is that knowledge is power.

If I wanted to further myself in life and have control over my destiny, I knew I had to get an education.

At that point in my life, my options were quite limited because of my poor performance in high school, but I knew that opportunity began with education. My transition from the army to education was an interesting one.

During my first semester at a junior college, I enrolled in a program called Interdisciplinary Studies. Their structure made learning fun again because often we would mix an English class with philosophy or history. I thrived in that environment. After one semester and some renewed confidence, I transferred to Eastern Illinois University (EIU), where I had a contingent of friends already there with a space for me in their house—and my own room!

At EIU, I immersed myself in the collegiate and social life. I embraced sports and all the intramural competitions, as well as the parties. As a junior, I was a candidate for the student body president. I lost but nonetheless still served in student government. My defeat was a humbling experience, but it taught me the importance of humility and hard work. Just as important as being president were the contributions I was able to make through my service to others.

In my senior year, I was fascinated with the idea of sponsorship after attending a conference in Chicago. I applied that knowledge to Eastern Illinois and created an event for our triathlon club. It was an indoor triathlon. I actually paid more attention to this entrepreneurial endeavor than I did to my classes in my senior year, but I was having a blast.

I organically found my career and purpose at the same time: creating opportunities for people to have fun in a healthy environment, while raising funds for great charities.

It has continued to morph since then, and I have learned more about myself.

You, and your purpose, should always be evolving. Later, we will be working on your purpose/mission statement. And, of course, since we are in this together, I will share mine.

Now, take some time away from this book. Get that note pad or laptop back out. Or use the blank pages at the back of this book.

Write a personal biography about your True Self—your weaknesses, passions, motivations, and the inspirations that helped shape your life.

Get to work.

Be honest with yourself.

...

Did you do it? Not so fun? Are you the person you want to be? It is okay if you are not. Nobody is perfect. We are all unmanifest energy able to create who we are based on our decisions in each moment.

Am I good or bad? It is not binary—We can be both, depending on our actions. We have all made bad decisions, but does that make us a bad person?

When I turned 50, I had a double fusion on my vertebrae in my lower back. I was laid up in bed for a few weeks. It gave me the time to reflect on what I wanted for the rest of my life. I made the decision to go back to school and get my Master's Degree so I could manage a boutique resort on a beach somewhere with warm weather.

That decision to keep reinventing myself opened so many more doors for me—because I chose to create opportunity for myself through education. It was a conscious decision to manifest my destiny.

Lots of people questioned the decision to go back to school at age 50, when I was never a great student in the first place. People close to me were worried. If I had listened, I would not have learned so much or created the life I wanted to build for myself.

I have found that uneducated people in our society look to blame others for their lack of progress in life. They often refer to "illegals stealing our jobs" and "invading our land." But didn't we Americans do just that only a few hundred years ago from the Native Americans who had lived here for centuries?

I believe that the blame on immigrants is misplaced. Folks that decide to educate themselves are literally creating many more valuable career opportunities for themselves. America is the land of opportunity for entrepreneurs.

We are free thinkers and doers. It is not others taking away our jobs, but rather technology is taking them away through automation. Nobody "owes" anyone a factory job. The sooner we, as a society, learn and accept that, the sooner our citizens can move forward to better paying positions by using our creative skills and our intelligence. With education and knowledge, we create power: Knowledge is Power—the power to choose and create our destiny.

Deep Dive

EXISTENTIALISM
—DAN BEEMAN

Now, I have set the tone for the book: Our goals. Our Inspirations. Honest Self Introspection.

Next, I will give you a bit of information about the meaning of existentialism and some of the concepts and terms that will get us started on our journey together.

ex·is·ten·tial·ism
A philosophical theory or approach that emphasizes the existence of the individual person as a free and responsible agent determining their own development through acts of will.

Existentialism is very straightforward. It is focused on human existence.

It is the lens we will use to look at aspects of the human existence in our essays.

"It is that every one of us, as an individual, is responsible—responsible for what we do, responsible for who we are, responsible for the way we face and deal with the world, responsible, ultimately, for the way the world is. It is, in a very short phrase, the philosophy of 'no excuses!'

Life may be difficult; circumstances may be impossible. There may be obstacles, not least of which are our own personalities, characters, emotions, and limited means or intelligence. But, nevertheless, we are responsible. We cannot shift that burden onto God, or nature, or the ways of the world. If there is a God, we choose to believe." —Robert C. Solomon

There are and were many noted existential philosophers.

Søren Kierkegaard refers to existentialism as a life that is filled with passion, self-understanding, and commitment.

For Friedrich Nietzsche, to really "exist" is to manifest your talents and virtues, "becoming the person you really are."

That is what existentialism is all about. We are responsible for ourselves. There are no excuses.

To me, the main pillars of existentialism are:

1. Free will
2. Passion
3. Accountability

Free will and the individual. Man can reason and act according to reason or without reason. He can think and act. It is not the thinking that makes us human, it is the actions we decide to take that make up our experience.

To the existentialist, "I think, therefore, I am" is inadequate. It might sound more like this, "What I do is who I am," or as Aristotle said, "I am what I repeatedly do, excellence then, is not an act but a habit."

Passion. Passion is the energizing source that creates purpose. Our purpose comes from the actions we take according to our passions. Passion gives meaning to existence. Passion does not come from reason. It is ephemeral and fundamental to our existence.

The central role of passion is opposed to the usual philosophical emphasis on reason and rationality. Instead, the emphasis is on a passionate commitment. For the existentialist, to live is to live passionately.

Accountability. Free will is freedom, but every action has a consequence. We are each accountable for our actions.

Existentialists are concerned with personal freedom, both political freedom and free will. This is central to Kierkegaard and Sartre, but not so much for Nietzsche and Heidegger. The relationship between freedom and reason is particularly at issue. Traditionally, acting "rationally" is said to be free, while acting out of emotion is considered being a "slave to one's passions."

The existentialists suggest that we live best, and are most

ourselves, in terms of passion. Kierkegaard's notion of "passionate commitment" is central. The special meaning of the term, "existence," is first defined by Kierkegaard to refer to a life that is filled with passion, self-understanding, and commitment.

For Nietzsche, to really exist is to manifest our talents and virtues—"becoming the person you really are." The key component of existentialism's general sensibility is Descartes's assertation that "I think, therefore I am," which is a problem, not a solution, to the question of existence. The existentialists challenge the idea that human existence is so connected with thinking.

Existentialism urges us to live our lives to the fullest, although what this means will take a variety of forms.

Friedrich Nietzsche

Deep Dive

The history of existential philosophy dates to Socrates, who died in 399 BC. Socrates believed the best way for people to live was to focus on the pursuit of virtue rather than the pursuit of material wealth. His principal method of reasoning was questioning.

He died as Jesus died, condemned to death by a consensus of his peers.

It reminds me of this quote I read in one of my favorite books, *The Confederacy of Dunces,* "When a true genius appears in the world, we will know him by this sign; all of the dunces were lined up in a confederacy against him."

Other noted philosophers like Kant, Kafka, and Dostoyevsky furthered existentialist theories up to the more recent contributions from Jean-Paul Sartre, who died in 1980. Sartre's primary work was exploring the concept that people, as humans, are "condemned to be free." We have free will and will make the decisions that impact our lives.

Sartre was particularly influential after World War II, when the world was changing quickly and dramatically. He readily acknowledged that he was most interested in studying the self in the environment of his times—not past or future but his specific era of thinking from 1945–1980.

For contextual purposes, in 1980, when he died, the cell phone had not yet been invented. His life was not easy compared with today's modern conveniences.

Jean-Paul Sartre

One of the founding principles of existentialism is that existence precedes essence. What you are—your essence—is a result of your choices. Your existence as a human being is first, rather than the reverse. Essence is not a given destiny. You are what you make yourself to be.

In other words, Manifest Destiny. We are what we make of our lives. Not, "How is life treating you?" but "How are you treating your life?"

Existentialism is a movement, not a set of doctrines. It is neither religious nor anti-religious. It is not political or against political ideologies.

Of the leaders or "modern existentialists," Kierkegaard was a pious Christian, while Nietzsche and Sartre were atheists. Kierkegaard despised politics, Sartre was a Marxist, Camus was a humanitarian, and Heidegger was a Nazi.

Of them, the only true existentialist was Sartre, who coined the term existentialism. He pursued the idea that "We make ourselves."

The existentialists all possessed an eccentric commonality, and each of them took individuality in a different direction.

Of all philosophers, existentialists are the most geared toward thinking about our needs and expectations. Despite European origins, existentialism is perfectly suited to contemporary American thought, because our culture is very focused on our personal happiness and needs—Humanistic Egocentrics.

Since this book is a philosophical study of humans written by humans, it is important to give the context and origins of existentialist thought, the leaders, and their philosophies.

I acknowledge the past thinkers and am inspired by them but am much more interested in the exploration of ourselves than the ideas of others.

Our introspective study together—the Socratic method of understanding the nature of man—will be conducted by asking our own questions of ourselves. A deep, internal dive, rather than studying the history of the theory and the proponents of existentialism.

I will ask you questions at the end of each essay and encourage you to look at things through the lens of existentialism: What would the existentialists say?

We will call this enterprise a Modern Existential Inquiry.

***

One note of caution, the existentialists wrote of life being difficult for many of them. We must recognize that they wrote of their personal experiences in the time and place in which they lived. Modern conveniences through technology have vastly improved living conditions in many places, especially in the USA in the past 40 years. What we now consider necessities would have been unfathomable luxuries just 40 years ago.

While we have modern conveniences through technology, which puts all needed information at our fingertips through the Internet, we also have some challenges in this journey. Now, we will explore some of the challenges and distractions.

DISTRACTIONS
—DAN BEEMAN

IMMEDIACY OF SOCIAL MEDIA

I have chosen to include essays on existential topics that human beings have pondered for centuries. These are issues many of us have also considered and editorialized in social media.

This is my attempt to step back from the immediate response cycle common in social media, and to deeply articulate my thoughts with my best attempt at objectivity on the subjects.

I have found the social media space inadequate for introspection for a few reasons.

1. People want to respond immediately without fully digesting the shared material.

2. People defend their existing position or opine without accepting new information.

3. People use different techniques for debate: Red herring (change the subject), attack the messenger (you are dumb), or ignore (disengage).

4. None of these further knowledge or understanding of existential questions.

The spewing of venom through relative anonymity in social media is also a common and growing concern that reduces the viability of it as a platform for intellectual discussions.

Therefore, I wrote this book to inspire deeper thought and authentic dialogue among readers and to inspire greater understanding of the issues, ourselves, and other human beings.

This quote came to me as I was pondering what to do with my thoughts when I found social media to be an inadequate platform and a place where opinion screams louder than truth.

It is the impetus for this book.

"Permitting ignorance is empowering it
Repeating ignorance perpetuates it
Sharing it enough validates it
Silence in the face of it is irresponsible
Truth should be sought, confirmed, and shared."

—Dan Beeman

With greater understanding of ourselves and the issues we are investigating, we can become more fully realized human beings. What we will do is explore our thinking with our words. I will challenge your thinking by sharing ours to see how it coalesces or differs. Hopefully that will lead to more conscious introspection and, eventually, more purposeful living.

PRIORITIES

Let's face it. We have lots of distractions.

Subconsciously, many of us wonder about our human existence on Earth—where we came from, why, how, and when. We also wonder where we are going or what happens after life.

We say "subconsciously" because in this "information age," during our non-working hours, we are also constantly distracted with information that focuses on the immediate— both internally and externally.

Internally—Am I hungry, thirsty, happy, sad, tired, lonely,

horny, hot, cold, etc.?

Externally—How many devices am I using now that either entertain or interrupt my clear thinking—TV? Radio? Amazon Echo, Google Home, social media? According to *Forbes Magazine,* we are exposed to 5,000+ advertisements per day. Wow!

As human beings with life expectancies of less than 100 years, our perspective is naturally short-sighted in relation to the age of the planet (4+ billion years) and the age of our species (200,000 years).

We also need to explore other questions.

What "quadrant" am I spending most of my conscious time in?

Am I proactive with my planning or subject to focusing on immediate gratification?

How does my desire for immediate gratification affect my choices in my activities?

What is society telling me about how to think and how to act?

All these internal and external messages constantly being processed by our brain occupy its capacity. They overload it. This constricts our ability to ponder important existential questions during our non-working hours.

Existential issues are often perceived as unimportant because they do not help accomplish the urgent tasks at hand. Therefore, they are repressed into a region that is largely unexplored.

Wait! How are we so distracted? Why?

Let's break up the day in thirds—sleeping, working, and other. If we are not able to consciously ponder existential questions during 2/3rds of our day, that means we are reduced to pondering important issues in a small percentage of time.

What is in the "other" 1/3 of our waking/non-working life?

Family, social activity, nourishment, education, worship, exercise, volunteering, entertainment, social media, television, radio, movies, podcasts, books, sports, grooming, planning, daydreaming, etc.

Of that 1/3, reflection sits in Quadrant 2: Not Urgent/ Important. This is the quadrant where people spend the least amount of time. This puts it behind Urgent/Important and Urgent/Unimportant. In 3rd place...not good.

Many things that people perceive to be important because they are urgent are actually unimportant, yet they still get much more time and attention than philosophical analysis of self. Urgent is not necessarily important. They should not be confused with each other.

Read that one back again and take a minute to think about it.

Urgent is not the same thing as important. There is a big difference.

Wait, it gets worse. The 4th quadrant is the tempting space of emptiness. It is Not Urgent/Not Important. It is a place of self-pacification. It is a place we go or stay because it is safe—to retreat from the "torrent of cognition." So we do things like watch TV or scroll through social media because it allows us to stop thinking while being entertained. We love the comfort of this space and go there more often than we want to admit.

Here are the quadrants.

	URGENT	NOT URGENT	
IMPORTANT	Q1 CRISES EMERGENCIES	Q2 PREVENTION PLANNING IMPROVEMENT	**IMPORTANT**
NOT IMPORTANT	Q3 INTERRUPTIONS	TIME WASTERS	**NOT IMPORTANT**
	URGENT	NOT URGENT	

In addition to pondering existentialism being labeled as Unimportant, are the constant societal media and marketing messages we receive from all the stimulus around us.

Those messages take advantage of our desire for approval/satisfaction/success/happiness to get our attention to buy or consume a product or service. This is reinforced by a culture within our society that depends on growth (sales of more products and services) to enable the sustainability of their growth.

Tash Pericic discusses these in the last essay of the book. How can we use this time to pause, think, and change?

***

Now, since we have established there is little time and barely any priority for introspection and exploration of existential questions, why is it important to explore these issues?

Why should we seek answers to questions that we actively avoid—both consciously and subconsciously?

Because, it is gnawing at our subconscious!

Our desire to understand our role on Earth and our place in the universe occasionally surfaces when we gaze at the stars in the sky on a clear night.

Or hike in nature.

Or scuba dive.

Or explore Google Earth.

Or when we are forced to shelter in place due to a global pandemic like Covid-19.

These experiences allow us to peel back the curtain of distraction and open the door to a semi-objective perception and authentic cognition.

Why?

Because reflection and introspection are important. Important because they help us understand ourselves better.

"Everything is preceded by the mind. The quality of your life is the quality of your mind. If your mind is agitated, the whole world is known to you as various forms of agitation. If your mind is quiet and peaceful, which takes considerable effort, the whole world is seen to be permeated with quietude and peace," says noted yoga instructor and thinker, Jason Bowman.

Jason Bowman practices Vipassana meditation to calm the mind. He says, "The practice teaches a person how to shift identification away from the torrent of cognition and onto the thing that can observe cognition change."

Vipassana, which means to see things as they really are, is one of India's most ancient techniques of meditation. It was rediscovered by Gotama Buddha more than 2,500 years ago and was taught by him as a remedy for universal ills, i.e., an art of living. This non-sectarian technique aims for the total eradication of mental impurities and the resultant highest happiness of full liberation.

According to Wikipedia, Vipassana is a way of self-transformation through self-observation. It focuses on the deep interconnection between mind and body, which can be experienced directly by disciplined attention to the physical sensations that form the life of the body, and that continuously interconnect and condition the life of the mind. It is this observation-based, self-exploratory journey to the common root of mind and body that dissolves mental impurity, resulting in a balanced mind full of love and compassion.

Vipassana is a wonderful practice, but it claims to enable objectivity.

Deep Dive

I disagree. It may help one become *more objective*, but total, pure objectivity is impossible.

However, one must be careful with ego in relation to yoga or meditation. Bowman also says, "Using meditation as an Identity ('I am a Yogi') is perversely oxymoronic because the actual practice itself is used to help us dismantle the ornaments we hang out ourselves."

HUMAN WEAKNESS/EGO

There are also other factors limiting reflection, which we will explore in this book: The current iteration of human beings is not a fully evolved species.

We want to think we are objective.

We want to think that we are right.

We are fallible.

We desire simple, concrete answers and solutions.

We seek approval.

We want happiness.

We want success and to be perceived as successful.

Most of us are object-oriented versus subject-oriented.

Object orientation says, "What others think about the image I project is more important than the truth I know about my authentic self." —Deepak Chopra

Ego is dangerous. It warps our reality and affects our relationship with ourselves, our fellow human beings, and planet Earth.

Object orientation is the reliance on other opinions about me more than I value my own opinion of myself. The ego embraces object-orientation because it thrives on the feedback of others.

***

The opposite of object orientation is subject orientation. Subject orientation says that I trust my knowledge of myself. My opinion of myself is all that really matters: Others may judge my outward appearance, but only I know the content of my character.

As Martin Luther King, Jr. said, "I have a dream that my four little children will one day live in a nation where they will not be judged by the color of their skin, but by the content of their character."

Ever since I developed a hereditary skin disease called vitiligo, which causes a loss of pigmentation and skin color, I feel less connected to my epidermis and vanity and more connected to who I am on the inside.

I feel less concerned with what others say about me and more concerned about how I feel about myself. Believe it or not, despite the visual blemishes, it is incredibly liberating.

CONTEXT/PERSPECTIVE/SUBJECTIVITY

Next, our study of existentialism cannot begin until we understand our subjective paradigm.

This subjective paradigm is the lens through which we experience the world.

There are several levels to subjectivity. Each level multiplies the difference between what we think about something and how others think about it.

Perception—seeing, feeling, smelling, touching, or hearing something.

Processing—receiving that information and deciding the priority of it.

Coalescing—integration of information with previous understanding.

Communicating—sharing the perspective with others.

Receiving—our intended message is received by another subjective person.

And the cycle continues, for every single person with every single message—verbal and non-verbal.

The perspective of past behavior is warped and often inaccurate for many reasons—duration of time elapsed, biased interpretation, and our unreliable memory, which deteriorates over time.

Think about that for a moment.

Our view of the past comes from a distorted lens (paradigm). It is an organically myopic view further tainted by factors of time, age, and an imperfect brain.

However, our future behavior is dictated by our experiences in the past—whether those experiences were recent or distant history, or evolved through books and stories based on how they were interpreted at the time, according to the story-teller.

So, here we are, in the present, focused on trying to objectively study the present existential issues facing mankind. Yet, we are influenced by our pre-existing perceptions of the "nature" of man, the stories of our culture, our ego, our weakness of the mind, our lack of objectivity, and our paradigms.

We all have some perspective on how we think and feel about the following, apparent, inherent contradictions:

We tend to think that humankind is either mostly good/bad, kind/evil, moral/immoral, motivated/lazy, perfect/flawed, special/common, objective/subjective, generous/selfish, evolved/primitive, evolving/end product, the center of universe who is meant to rule all/member of a living community subject to natural law.

We tend to think Earth is mostly a living thing that is either communicative/silent, giving/taking, dangerous/safe, aging/ageless, sustainable/unsustainable, volatile/calm, enchanting/ordinary, unique/ordinary, and made for mankind/autonomous.

How we get along with each other as human beings and our relationship with the planet depends on the premise we choose, according to the stories we believe about our true nature.

Mind you, these are not mutually exclusive attributes: If you are one, can't you be the other?

No, you can be both good/bad, etc. We are all shades of grey on the spectrum of black and white. I have been both many times.

So, what am I? What are you?

But we also tend to at least shade in one direction or the other on the questions about our perspectives on mankind and Earth.

As Deepak Chopra says, "We are all unmanifest energy, organically seeking our authentic self."

Stephen Covey quotes William George Jordan, "Into the hands of every individual is given a marvelous power for good or evil, the silent unseen unconscious influence of his life. This is the constant radiation of what man really is, not what he pretends to be."

We are all a blend of many changing attributes, characteristics, and perspectives based on new absorption of information and experiences.

The un-stubborn tend to be fluid and open to new information. The porous sponge absorbs. Mankind has evolved because we have adapted to our environment.

Duality is part of human nature. In all of us exists darkness and light, good and evil.

POLITICS AND RELIGION

Our lens is further obscured by a couple of other institutions through the applications of their ideologies. Politics and religion expose and magnify those dividing inclinations in people.

They are both unifying and polarizing. They unify one group who believe but polarize themselves from others who disagree with their perspective.

When utilizing fear as a primary tool of support, cable news channels use established agendas to push ideologies. Therefore, a further divide may occur for both sides of the spectrum as respective narratives are pushed. This is true for both sides of the spectrum.

Fortunately, existentialism is not about politics or religion. It is about the individual.

However, we must remember that our political and religious beliefs impact our perspective—they may also distort the lens and impact the human existence.

Think about these quotes and people that support and reinforce those ideas.

"Nobody knows the system better than me, which is why I alone can fix it," Donald Trump told the Republican National Convention, June 21, 2016.

"Only our religion can promise eternal life," many religions attest.

Both contradict existential ideology. Both undermine the power of the autonomy of the individual and affect free will. They both want the individual to cede the responsibility of the self to someone or something else.

They are saying, "Without me or our religion, you cannot achieve your ultimate destiny."

We are interested in exploring human behavior and purpose because it interests us as humans currently living a human existence.

STORIES

The future of mankind is just pure speculation. An informed speculation, certainly, based on the past and cumulative stories regarding the experience of mankind on Earth. But we can't accurately predict the future.

We know that we lean on our past life experiences and the historical stories from our culture, which we choose to believe, in order to support our perspectives Then, the stories start to become a self-perpetuating cycle of belief reinforcement until opinions are considered factual, since they are repeated and reinforced so often that they eventually become accepted as, yep, universally true.

But are they really? Does everybody agree on any one thing?

Daniel Quinn posits a theory in *Ishmael*. He says that there was a separation of people about 10,000 years ago when the Leavers (hunter/gatherers) were destroyed by the Takers (agriculturalists). He says that Mother Culture has convinced mankind that man is above natural law. Agriculturalists believed this to mean that Earth was made for man to rule. Mankind has taken that to the next logical step—that we can do what we please with Earth to satisfy our needs and gain pleasure: aka happiness.

This is one story in a great book that I recommend. The Bible is another story that I highly recommend.

They are both stories. Read them. Come to your own conclusions.

UNIVERSALITY

So, if the lens with which we view the world is distorted,

unclear, subjective, and subject to change, how can we identify universal truth? Does it exist?

Mankind is not universally anything, except from our common generic, physical structure. We are diverse physically, ethnically, educationally, economically, spiritually, philosophically, and geographically. We all see things according to our unique, subjective paradigm.

Laws – Natural VS. Man

Laws of science, which were thought to be universal laws, are simply educated guesses. No law of science can ever be a universal law because we do not have universal experiences.

Our knowledge of the universe is minute compared to what is possible, so that we must remain ignorant of any universal laws about the universe (Everything is subjective). Therefore, it is not reasonable to expect to know universal laws. If they do exist, we will never know them.

Universal statements, which are called "laws" of science, are based upon a limited number of observations. This is called induction. Induction is always a logical fallacy because universal conclusions based upon a limited number of observations can never be conclusive. Therefore, no law of science can ever be relied on as true.

We need to be ready to revise our laws as we experience more and novel observations, which will force us to revise or discard our laws of nature.

A law in science is a generalized rule to explain a body of observations in the form of a verbal or mathematical statement. Scientific laws (also known as natural laws) imply a cause and effect between the observed elements and must always be applied under the same conditions. In order to be scientific law, a statement must describe some aspect of the universe and be based on repeated experimental evidence. Scientific laws may be stated in words, but many are expressed as mathematical equations. Laws are widely accepted as true, but new data can lead to changes in a law or to exceptions to the rule.

Sometimes laws are found to be true under certain conditions, but not others. For example, Newton's Law of Gravity holds true for most situations, but it breaks down at the sub-atomic level.

Our diversity led to evolution of mankind over time. The evolution of all species comes from diversity and adaptation.

For example, there may be a motivated real estate agent in California and a lazy waitress in Belize. Or it could be the other way around.

There could be a brilliant fisher and sailor in Tahiti, who can't read or write. Or there could be a scholar in London who can't swim, sail, or survive in nature.

Who is more "evolved" and how can they be considered "equal"?

"We hold these truths to be self-evident, that all men are created equal, that they are endowed by their Creator with certain unalienable Rights, that among these are Life, Liberty and the pursuit of Happiness." —Declaration of Independence

Our "equality" depends on how you define it. "Equal" from the standpoint of intellect, opportunity, or just in the eyes of God? We are unique with different skills and abilities. So, equality, like everything, is subjective.

PERCEPTIONS/CONTRADICTIONS

We will explore many issues with an intentional focus on contradictions, irony, and hypocrisy.

How two people see the same thing, but have a different view of it, is often the hypocrisy of contradiction. It magnifies the lens of the difference in people's perspectives. What you see depends on how you perceive it. Your perspective can and will change frequently as you receive more information.

How can our Declaration of Independence declare that all men are created equal, yet consider black slaves as "property"?

Why does a billionaire want to earn billions more and yet a Buddhist monk abstains from any material wealth to achieve happiness and success? Who is happier and more successful?

Why are people pro-life but support gun rights without restrictions, which results in the killing of innocent human beings?

Why are there slogans such as "If you want something done, do it yourself" and "Interdependence is the key to happiness"?

Why are religion and religious people considered "good" and yet religion is also considered the root of evil perpetrated by man in allegiance to his religious ideologies?

What is a better and more honest expression of cultural structures in society—Capitalism or Communism? Why?

Why is the public act of kneeling considered both honoring and disrespecting something at the same time by different people?

Was this planet designed for mankind and, therefore, mankind is the ruler of the planet to do with as we please?

Why do we say we love Earth, but our collective behavior destroys it at the same time?

What is the true nature of mankind—selfless or selfish?

If the United States is a "Christian nation," why is there a constitution that specifically, intentionally separates the church and state?

Hypocrisy. Duality. Humanity. Nuance. Existence.

Will we give you definitive, specific answers to these questions?

No. We only have our perspective. But we will help you think about them to help you make your choice for yourself.

***

I once told a friend that I'd found the key to happiness. I said, "The key to happiness is as simple as being connected and productive." He said, "for you." I laughed, then let it sink in. It really resonated and still does. It was only two words, but the most profound words I ever heard.

I never forgot it.

We are all individuals seeking our own path.

We all see things from a different lens. Our only human commonality is that we all have our own perspective.

Or everything is subjective to each individual.

Since we have reviewed the implications on how we see things and why, let's do an exercise applying some of our learning. With your subject-oriented lens on, take a few minutes and write down what you want to be in your life on Earth.

This is your **Individual Aspiration Statement.** It can and will change.

It might sound something like this:

"I want to be present in each moment by listening to others, pausing before responding, and living my life with integrity, while manifesting my destiny."

OR

"I want to create happiness wherever I go."

OR

"I want to explore every relationship in my life to either enhance it or end it."

OR

"I want to bring the message of my religion to all I meet."

OR

"I want to find my purpose and live it."

∗∗∗

ASSUMPTIONS

Based on everything we have shared above, for the purposes of the essays, here are our assumptions. Think of this as the amount of air in your tank, your fins, mask, and other equipment that we will take on the dive together.

Mankind is flawed and not a fully evolved species.

Our mind, memory, and scope of comprehension are limited.

Our lens forces us to be subjective in our thinking, even though we try to be as objective as possible.

We are organically hedonistic as a species—motivated by seeking pleasure and avoiding pain.

We are self-centered and mostly focused on our own success and happiness.

We are distracted by the culture we live in that interferes with discovering ourselves.

We live in an object-oriented culture that is more concerned with the opinion of others than how we authentically feel about ourselves.

Most people go through life without doing the work to take the deep dive—to understand and live according to our authentic nature.

Most people think that their goal in life is to be happy without accountability to the impact of their behavior on all other life forms, including the planet.

PART 2
THE SELF

Deep Dive

PART 2: ESSAYS

This section contains a series of essays loosely connected under four categories: Self, Society/Humanity, Gods/Religion, and Earth. Some essays touch on one or more subjects. We will begin with an internal exploration of ourselves.

Do you have a creed or document meant to direct your actions according to your beliefs? I wrote this for my Godson and presented it to his parents on the day of his baptism in 1992. My goal was to provide him some inspiration for how to embrace and live life fully.

I will:

* Live my life fully, seeking new experiences every day through people and places without falling prey to a monotonous, routine existence.

* Understand that I am a part of a greater being and am a

79

special person in the eyes of God, who can make a difference in the world by loving the people around me.

* Challenge myself and others to grow and learn; to diversify myself through art, literature, and music, while maintaining balance in my life.

* Follow the footsteps of Christ and lead others down the same path by inspiring those I love and loving those who inspire me.

* Respect my parents and listen to them, for their wisdom is of experience and is imparted to me out of love.

* Look at the world through the eyes of a child by appreciating the little things like laughter, nature, and honesty.

* Live my life with integrity, knowing that I am only as good as my word.

* Thank God daily for all the gifts he has given me, not physical or materialistic things but spiritual, emotional, and intellectual.

Some of these suggestions may or may not resonate with you. Like everything else in this book, take and absorb what you want and apply it as you wish.

Our first essay will kick off a series of exercises that will help us understand ourselves better and how we view ourselves in relation to other important entities impacting our existence.

In the end of the book, following our reflections and the

exercises, we will have a much better sense of our self and our purpose, which will help us better understand how we want to live our lives.

WHAT AM I DOING HERE?
—DAN BEEMAN

Central to a pursuit of self-knowledge is how I see things (perceptions) and how am I spending my time (actions). How do I balance my talents, find my purpose, provide for my family, and serve others or God?

Your Dharma, or *raison d'etre* is the intersection of your passion, mission, profession, and vocation. This is also the intersection of your calling as a productive member of society who supports your fellow citizens, community, family, and self. How you prioritize those four relationships dictates the path you choose.

For example, a father of seven children may not do what he loves because he is prioritizing his ability to get paid for certain work in order to provide for his family. This was the case with my father. He loved broadcasting and did that while in college and the military service. However, he got married and had seven kids. His priorities changed.

Since we have already completed our biographies and we understand that we all have unique perspectives, we will now diagram our own unique perspectives.

One way to do this is by drawing Venn Diagrams.

Venn Diagrams visually show how different things interrelate.

Venn di·a·gram

A diagram representing mathematical or logical sets pictorially as circles or closed curves within an enclosing rectangle (the universal set), common elements of the sets being represented by the areas of overlap among the circles.

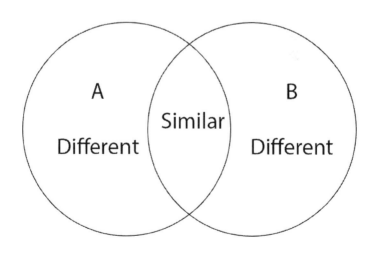

Have you reflected on your priorities? How has that affected your decisions? Are you able to adjust or are you stuck in the current situation because you are afraid to change? Or afraid of failure? Have you and your family become accustomed to the material benefits of "What I can be Paid For" instead of "What I love" or "Good at Serving Humanity"?

Since our journey begins with self, it is important to assess how we see the relationships among ourselves, society, religion, and Earth.

To reinforce how we are all different with a subjective perspective, we have an exercise to do together.

In the following diagram, we show one of the ways people see their relationships with the four broad categories impacting your existence. As you can see,

84

this does not consider God or religion. Yours might.

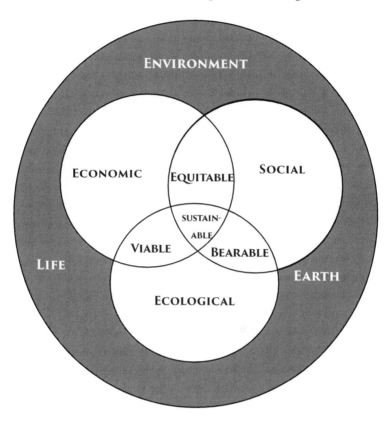

How do you see the relationship between the four main entities?

Take out a piece of paper or use a blank page in the back of the book and draw four circles containing the words, *Self, Humankind, Earth,* and *the Gods,* then add as many other circles with words as you want to create your own Venn Diagram.

Don't be constrained. Add or subtract circles as desired with categories or words that make sense to you in drawing your diagram. Take your time.

Challenge Questions:

What is the center? How do the circles interact? Is there a confluence?

After you finish, ask yourself if this has changed over time in your life?

How does it compare with others?

How does your view of their relationship affect the way you think and act?

EMOTIONAL INTELLIGENCE
AND THE GAP
—DAN BEEMAN

"Between stimulus and response, there is a space. And in that space is our power to choose our response. In our response lies our growth and our freedom."

—Victor E. Frankl

We are surrounded by stimulation during every waking hour of our lives. Remember, Jason Bowman calls it a "torrent of cognition," which not only impacts our analysis of self but much more frequently forces us to navigate the gap between stimulus and response.

Our emotional intelligence—that maturity of thought that helps us moderate the space in the gap, is defined by how we navigate the gap.

Deep Dive

This space, this navigation of the space, is what makes us uniquely human. We are not animals. We can choose a response. However, the choice is a mental muscle we must exercise, called discipline.

A lazy mind with no discipline reacts instantly, and often defensively, to support a previously held position.

"In the space between stimulus (what happens) and how we respond, lies our freedom to choose. Ultimately, this power to choose is what defines us as human beings. We may have limited choices, but we can always choose. We can choose our thoughts, emotions, moods, our words, our actions; we can choose our values and live by principles. It is the choice of acting or being acted upon."

—Stephen R. Covey

"The ability to subordinate an impulse to a value is the essence of a proactive person," says Covey.

Proactive people subordinate feelings to value and act in accordance with the value when responding to stimulus.

We often see this in a social media debate. People respond without really listening, are unable (or unwilling) to subordinate an impulse, and often reiterate the same talking points they are comfortable with, instead of actively listening with the hope of gaining knowledge and furthering a healthy dialogue.

Navigating space begins with active listening. Covey calls this proactivity or "First Seek to Understand before Being

Understood."

Awareness of the gap and active management of our actions help us manage our responses and relationships to reach greater emotional maturity.

This awareness, imbued with empathy and supported by values, enhances communications and supports better relationships with others.

But, what if I am not always aware and filled with empathy? What if I am not living according to my values?

What if I am an 18-year-old soldier struggling to understand my purpose? What if I am a teenage girl grappling with body issues? What if I am a catfished young man?

What if the other person in the relationship is not playing by the same rules of awareness, empathy, and values? How do I square the value of competition and nurturing?

Chopra says, "Our thinking and our behavior are always in anticipation of a response. It is therefore fear-based."

I disagree with Chopra. It doesn't mean that fear is not powerful. It *is* powerful, which is why politicians often use it to further their agenda.

If we are subject-oriented, value-based, and principle-centered, our behavior will organically be honorable, so there should be no fear in our actions.

However, if we are not living according to our values and principles, we are living hypocritically.

Freedom of choice. Free will. Freedom. These are all fundamental to existentialism. You get to choose your actions.

Challenge Questions:

Are you a reactive person?

What are the ways you can increase the space of your gap between stimulus and response?

Do you think, *How am I treating my life?* or *How is life treating me?*

Do you live in fear?

What would existentialists say about the gap?

COACHING: HOW HELPING OTHERS HELPED ME
—SIMONA KSOLL

Twelve years ago, I had the carpet ripped out from under my feet. It was the day before Valentine's when my then-husband dropped the bomb that he wanted to separate.

Two weeks later, he moved out.

I went into a fog, trying to come to terms with the fact that my shaky marriage of fifteen years had finally fallen apart for good. Between three weekly therapy sessions and endless hours on the phone, crying, my life was on autopilot.

My weekdays started morphing into each other. I'd pop a tranquilizer with my morning coffee to be able to function at work, closing my office door after each meeting to have a meltdown, and then putting on more make-up to hide the fact that I'd just bawled my eyes out.

I started exercising excessively three times a day. Two hours prior to work and one after.

I dropped twenty pounds.

I got Botox for the first time to make myself feel better.

My colleagues asked me what fabulous diet I was on and complemented me on my svelte body and good looks.

I never told them what was really going on.

Fast forward a few months, the fog finally started to lift.

With the help of my therapist, I had started to put the broken pieces of me back together.

For the first time in years, I asked myself what I wanted to do, not how could I bend over backwards and squeeze myself into a box so that my husband would love me.

The answer I got was a vacation. I booked a trip to Mexico and decided to enroll in a yoga teacher training. This was the beginning of my transformation.

One morning as we were coming out of a meditation, I opened my eyes and I saw the beautiful Caribbean ocean in front of me. The rays of the sun made the water appear to shimmer in a gorgeous golden light, and at this moment of stillness, I heard a voice speak to me: *Simona, you have to move here.*

I remember the feeling of peace coming over me, a deep knowing of truth, and as I was reveling in it, I thought, *Yes, I want this.*

Until the next thought came. *How is this ever going to happen?*

Enter the Universe. It always brings you what you need when you need it. There were five women in the training, one of them was a transformational coach. At the time, I had no idea what a coach was. We started talking and I decided to work with her. In one of our sessions, I had a bigger breakthrough than in seven years of therapy.

I was stunned, and I knew I wanted more. My coach recommended I investigate a year-long personal development program. It was a big investment for me at the time, and I was scared to spend so much money on myself. But I did it despite the fear.

Little did I know that this program would answer my question of *How is this ever going to happen?*

I learned the skills of coaching and how to build a portable business that would allow me to move.

But I still wasn't there.

There was another obstacle, the most powerful of all: my own mind-set. My fears, my beliefs around being good enough, being deserving enough, and being worthy enough.

Enter the Universe, again. In this program, I met a woman who gave me a recording of a man she had just started to listen to. She encouraged me to study his teachings and go to one of his live events.

After listening to the recording, I knew I was in. I booked a ticket to the East Coast to see him and signed up to work with him privately. The investment was more than a brand new car.

Talk about scary. And again, I got exactly what I needed when I needed it.

After a year and a half of being mentored by him, he said something that lit the proverbial match for me. I realized that to get the result, I had to apply the concepts I was studying with him in my own life.

One of them was practicing my faith and let it be my guiding beacon of light instead of making decisions based in fear. Integrating the intellectual knowledge that the universe meets you in the field as soon as you step into it, not before, by actually doing it.

I was mad as hell at him when he told me, but it was exactly what I needed (thanks again, universe) to make the decision to move and take the first action step in this direction.

I signed a one-year lease for an apartment here in Playa del Carmen. That got the ball rolling.

The next logical step was to resign from my lucrative six-figure job at a Hollywood movie studio.

The day I walked into my boss's office, I was so terrified of committing financial suicide that he must have seen it on my face. He knew before I even said a word. I was torn between fainting and vomiting until I heard him say, "I'm so happy for you."

We sat down and talked about my exit strategy. Turns out, I stayed with the company for five more months as a full-time employee working from my apartment in Mexico. Previously unheard of in the company.

This allowed me to set up my coaching and consulting practice where I help others to do the same: make their big vision their reality.

As my clients embrace their gifts and share them with those who they are meant to be helping, it creates a huge ripple effect in the world.

And it all started with a voice that said, *Simona, you have to move here.*

It's interesting how you can always connect the dots looking back. I wouldn't be doing the work I'm doing today guiding others to step into their vision, had it not been for coaching.

It's a gift that keeps on giving, and it has transformed my life and the lives of my clients forever.

Challenge Questions:

Have you ever been on a career path that felt wrong?

If so, what did you do?

Are you ready to find your true purpose according to your passion?

Do you listen to and honor your inner voice?

Simona Ksoll is a Business Strategist & Personal Mentor to Entrepreneurs and Creatives, helping them tap into their inner superpowers so they can make their big vision their reality. A former global marketing executive at Sony Pictures, Simona supports her clients with subconscious belief change, neuroscientific re-patterning, teaching universal success principles and developing an individual business and/or lifestyle strategy that allows them to confidently step into their next chapter.

Meaning of Life for The Individual —Dan Beeman

Our ultimate objective with this book is to help you find authentic meaning in your life here on Earth—or, What are we doing here?

We have established that everything is subjective to everyone, depending on what they choose to believe—so the meaning of life to you is only about the meaning you give to life—how you live each day. Nobody else can answer this question for you or give you meaning in your life.

In order to find our individual meaning, we need to understand where your personal meaning comes from.

Socrates talked about living with virtue as the mechanism to provide meaning.

Kierkegaard talked about service to God as giving his life meaning.

Sartre believed that only by existing and acting a certain way do we give meaning to our lives. He also believed that life was lived in anguish, creating a miserable existence. This may have reflected the era in which he lived, which was devoid of many modern conveniences.

Covey talks about principle-centered living as the mechanism to provide meaning in his life.

Bobby McFerrin may best represent modern culture in his song "Don't worry. Be Happy."

These perspectives originate from some brilliant thinkers who have different definitions of what provides meaning in their lives—reinforcing the reality that meaning in your life is totally subjective.

Remember what my friend said, when I thought I had found the key to happiness?

"For you," he said.

Before we dive too deep, let's explore what most people think their goal in life is: To be happy. To be happy is to be content.

Is happiness fulfilling?

The problem with happiness as a goal, in and of itself, is that it is

Deep Dive

organically selfish and short-term. It may be more appropriate for people seeking happiness as a goal to say they are most interested in immediate gratification. If the goal is happiness, then why delay it? Why earn it? Who cares if my happiness comes at the expense of someone else or something else?

Sure, we all want to be happy because it feels good. But authentic happiness comes from having meaning in your life. So, the goal for people willing to dive deep is to have meaning, not just happiness, as an end goal.

In *The Alchemist*, we learn that what is important is not the end result but the journey.

Make sense? Okay, let's continue.

Drilling down deeper, meaning comes from purpose. Without purpose, it is impossible to have meaning in your life.

So how do we find our purpose? We must dive deeper.

Purpose comes from passion.

Passion is the energizing force for purpose. Living life with purpose creates a meaningful life.

Of course, it is possible to live without purpose or meaning. But that is just an existence.

We want, as the existentialists say, the "essence" of who we are.

Many people do not explore their interests, do not find passions, and live by "coasting through existence," according to the existentialists.

We are here exploring, diving deeper because we want to learn more about ourselves and our life meaning.

So, let's do it. Let's find our passion and use it to guide our personal mission.

Covey has a process, so we will use many of his tools to create our own mission statement.

It is called a mission statement because a mission requires action to fulfill the mission.

A personal mission statement is a declaration of an individual's purpose and path in life, emphasizing what is truly important to him or her. Personal mission statements were popularized when Covey suggested that people create them in his book *The 7 Habits of Highly Successful People.*

So, let's start with a simple question: What interests you? Does it inspire you? Maybe if that answer doesn't jump out to you, perhaps someone inspires you? What about them inspires you?

Take a minute to think about it. Jot down a few things. They can just be random words to help get you going.

Now, I am going to give an example using my mission statement.

Dan Beeman Personal Mission Statement

Use my passion for exploration to help myself and others, identify our purpose, and create a meaningful, enjoyable life.

The statement should have action to give it meaning. Your statement, like mine, will change over time.

Here is what it used to be when I first did the exercise over 30 years ago:

Creating opportunities for people to have fun in a healthy environment while raising funds for charities.

Now it is your turn.

Take your time.

Reflect.

Write your personal mission statement.

Challenge Questions:

Do you have passion in your life?

What is it?

Where does it come from?

Do you express it?

Do you have a purpose?

Are you living it?

What is your personal mission statement?

Deep Dive

My Expanded Mission Statement

To live a full life with integrity, creating dynamic environments by bringing vitality, compassion, and sincere interests in each moment.

To maintain balance while seeking to achieve goals in major life categories—spiritual, personal, physical, social, financial, intellectual, and family.

To parent with empathy and love.

To be the best person that I can be.

To accept the things I cannot change, the courage to change the things that I can, and the wisdom to know the difference.

To inspire others based on the way I live my life.

Now. You go. Without Fear. It can and will change.

Now, break down your Mission Statement into categories or add other ones that may be important to you. Here is my example:

I.   **Dan Beeman – Personal Goals**
  A.   Spiritual
    1.   Learn more about different religions.
    2.   Seek to understand and live life with purpose and integrity.
    3.   Become an active part of a spiritual community.
    4.   Create and live by a mutually agreed upon set of moral and ethical principles.
    5.   Live in harmony with Earth and others.
    6.   Seek to understand and develop a close relationship with God.
  B.   Financial
    1.   Maximize earning potential without compromising relationships or ethical standards.
    2.   Create and adhere to a budget that aligns with and supports other goals.
  C.   Career
    1.   Earn enough to support my family.
    2.   Give honest effort every day at work.
    3.   Identify and nurture enjoyable elements of your job.
    4.   Create a positive work environment and lead by example.
  D.   Personal
    1.   Work toward achieving every goal in every category daily.
    2.   Live by a personal mission statement that reflects goals.

3. Effectively balance goal-achieving activities.
4. Seek to inspire others and recognize those who inspire me.
5. Seek new experiences that support other goals daily.
6. Strengthen relationships with people who can help me reach my goals.
7. Participate in community, non-profit work.
8. Review all goals every day and act in every category every day.
E. Physical/fitness
1. Create specific goals and work daily to achieve them.
2. Live a healthy lifestyle, including eating well and taking vitamins daily.
3. Participate in athletics each week.
4. Compete in organized athletic events that require training and goal setting.
5. Limit alcohol consumption and drink responsibly.
F. Education/Intellectual
1. Pursue interests that stimulate creative thought and challenge my intellect.
2. Read often on subjects that support other goals.
3. Work to obtain knowledge and degrees that support financial and career goals.
4. Limit television viewing to education and sports programming of 10 hours per week.
G. Pleasure/Social
1. Find a soulmate who shares the same sense of adventure and passion for life.
2. Surround myself with positive, healthy, spiritual, and like-minded people.
3. Participate in social events that support other goals: book clubs, fitness activities, etc.

4.   Build community among friends by planning and organizing activities.

5.   Plan vacations that align with and support other goals.

H.   Family

1.   Be the best parent possible: positive, patient, loving, accepting.

2.   Identify and nurture positives.

3.   Share my life fully with the ones I love: dreams, fears, joy, pain, and goals.

4.   Seek to inspire the ones I love and prioritize them in my life.

5.   Communicate my love to those I love every day.

I chose eight categories for my life goals. My goals are meant to be a guide for you as you go through your goal-setting exercise. They are very personal but also very important. I highly recommend that you print yours out and put them in a place where you can review them daily—preferably in the morning in your bedroom as you gather your thoughts.

Now, it is your turn. Write your Personal Goals.

KICKING CANCER: HOW IT CHANGED MY LIFE
—TRACY NATHAN

It was a normal day in July 2001. I was living my best life working as a Concierge at the Ritz Carlton on Maui, taking guests out on horseback rides part time at Ironwood Ranch, and enjoying the slow, easy pace of the islands.

It was a perfect Maui weekend, and I was going out to breakfast with my friend Richard. We were waiting in line at our favorite spot called the Gazebo and out of nowhere, I passed out. I chalked it up to smoking too much dope, but I continued to feel unwell. I was losing weight, had a rash on my hand, and basically had no energy. I knew something was wrong.

After several doctor visits on the island with concerning test results, I immediately flew home to Los Angeles, where

I checked into Cedars Sinai Medical Center, met with the oncologist, and had a bone marrow biopsy, which resulted in a diagnosis of acute myelogenous leukemia. The date was August 9, 2001.

I will spare you all of the details, but after 36 bags of chemotherapy, 70 days on and off in the hospital, and a stem cell transplant, I am still here to tell my story, help others who are newly diagnosed, and make a difference whenever and wherever I can.

I am currently an Honored Teammate with The Leukemia and Lymphoma Society/Team and Training. I cofounded Team Soul Family with my adventure partner Maria Martell. Together a group of six dedicated ladies and I have raised money for research and completed both a half marathon in New Orleans and a hike in beautiful Yosemite. We are looking forward to our third event.

Has it been easy? No. We all have ups and downs, twists and turns, highs and lows. My priority is simple, to be grateful for every single day. It's all we all have.

You see, in the end, what I've really learned is that life ebbs and flows. My job is to simply go with it, learn the lesson, and then give it away.

Challenge Questions:

If you were faced with a life-threatening illness, how would you respond?

If you overcame a premature death, how would you live each day?

Should you live each day as though it is your last? What does that look like?

Would the existentialists say that you should be accountable for your life?

Tracy Nathan is a life lover currently residing in Southern California. She enjoys spending time with family/friends, being out in nature, and is extremely blessed to have a second chance at life.

THE DANGER OF EGO
—DAN BEEMAN

ego

a person's sense of self-esteem or self-importance
"a boost to my ego"

"Ego judges and punishes. Love forgives and heals."

—Anonymous

As we know, existentialism is a term coined by Jean-Paul Sartre. It is the study of the self as an individual. It says that we are the only ones responsible for our life—not the Gods, our parents, or our environment.

So, what is the self?

The self is an individual person as the object of its own reflective consciousness. Since self is a reference by a subject to the same subject, this reference is necessarily subjective.

Excessive love of self is very dangerous.

Ego is one of the worst "poisons." It can be more lethal to our well-being than anything else.

If we allow our ego to take over, we can destroy personal relationships, working relationships, and friendships.

An inflated ego has the power to make us see things differently than they are. Ego is the idea that the world revolves around us, that all good things that happened were meant for us, and all bad things that happened were meant to wound us.

Ego pushes people away and closes our minds. We stop listening to other people's ideas, we become critical of those around us, we become trapped and alone in our selfish desires.

What I have learned is that my ego gets in the way of living life to its fullest.

Personally, I have struggled with ego all my life. Amazingly, fortunately, at age 48, I got a skin disease called vitiligo. My skin began changing color. Just a little at first, but eventually, half of my body had no pigment in the skin, so I am half white (albino) and half colored (tan).

I noticed how people looked at me differently. Some judged. Others were curious.

I stopped gazing at myself in the mirror, looking at my superficial characteristics and began to try to look inward—not through the mirror, but in reflection. I began to see that who I am is about what I do, how I act, not what I look like.

It helped me see others with more empathy for none of us are perfect. It helped me see imperfection as what makes us human.

The opposite of ego is humility—not thinking less of yourself but thinking of yourself less.

The author after vitiligo

Deep Dive

Let's dive deeper and look at the collective American ego.

Most Americans think that we are the greatest country on Earth. We embrace the concept of American exceptionalism. American exceptionalism is one of three related ideas. The first is that the history of the United States is inherently different from that of other nations. In this view, American exceptionalism stems from its emergence from the American Revolution, thereby becoming what political scientist Seymour Martin Lip called "the first new nation" and developing a uniquely American ideology. "Americanism" is based on liberty, equality before the law, individual responsibility, republicanism, representative democracy, and laissez-faire economics.

This ideology itself is often referred to as "American exceptionalism." Second is the idea that the U.S. has a unique mission to transform the world. As Abraham Lincoln stated in the "Gettysburg Address" (1863), Americans have a duty to ensure, "government of the people, by the people, for the people, shall not perish from the earth." Third is the sense that the United States' history and mission give it a superiority over other nations.

The theory of the exceptionalism of the U.S. has developed over time and can be traced to many sources. French political scientist and historian Alexis de Tocqueville was the first writer to describe the country as "exceptional" in 1831 and 1840. The actual phrase "American exceptionalism" was originally coined by Soviet leader Joseph Stalin in 1929 as a critique of a revisionist faction of American communists who argued that the American political climate was unique, making it an "exception" to certain elements of Marxist theory. U.S. president Ronald Reagan is often credited with having crystallized this ideology in recent decades.

In Greek mythology, Icarus is the son of the master craftsman Daedalus, the creator of the labyrinth. Icarus and his father attempt to escape from Crete by means of wings that his father constructed from feathers and wax. Icarus's father warns him first of complacency and then of hubris, asking that he fly neither too low nor too high, so the sea's dampness will not clog his wings nor the sun's heat melt them. Icarus ignores his father's instructions not to fly too close to the sun; when the wax in his wings melts, he tumbled out of the sky and falls into the sea, where he drowns, sparking the idiom, "Don't fly too close to the sun."

The Icarus Syndrome: A History of American Hubris. Peter Beinart's provocative account of hubris in the American century describes Washington on the eve of three wars: World War I, Vietnam, and Iraq—three moments when American leaders decided they could remake the world in their image. Each time, leading intellectuals declared that the spread of democracy was inevitable. Each time, a president held the nation in the palm of his hand. And each time, a war conceived in arrogance brought tragedy and death to many American soldiers.

So why is ego the enemy? There are several reasons:
- Keeps you out of touch with reality.
- Creates unrealistic expectations and entitlement.
- Makes you dependent on external validation.

What are some ways to counteract the effects of ego?

- Do something, don't try to be somebody.
- Focus on effort, not outcomes.
- Make other people successful.

Where do you sit on this hierarchy?

Hierarchy of Ego Communication

"Creative people discuss ideas
Adventurous people talk about places
Materialistic people brag about things
Ignorant people spout opinions as facts
Superficial people gossip about each other
Selfish people just think about themselves."

—Dan Beeman,
adapted from a quote from Eleanor Roosevelt

Thank you to Wikipedia for some of the text included in this essay.

Challenge Questions:

Where do you fit in this hierarchy?

How much time is spent in each level?

How can you practice ways to counteract your tendencies toward ego centrism?

Do you believe in American exceptionalism?

Is American exceptionalism a compliment or insult?

What do the existentialists say about excessive ego?

FEAR
—DAN BEEMAN

Fear

An unpleasant emotion caused by the belief that someone or something is dangerous, likely to cause pain, or a threat.

"The only thing to fear is fear itself."

—Franklin D. Roosevelt

Fear is a powerful emotion.

It blocks the ability to absorb new information.

I learned several valuable lessons about fear as a scuba instructor. The first was when I was teaching mini-club scuba at Club Med to kids aged 4–12 in a pool with miniature equipment to fit their bodies.

I learned that fear is learned.

I would sit the kids on the side of the pool, and I would offer the chance for someone to go first, thinking that those courageous enough to go first would likely succeed and others would see their success and they would succeed too. However, if that person failed, then usually we had a lower rate of success with the rest of the kids. Failure from fear became self-perpetuating.

I learned that I shouldn't allow parents to watch because the kids would sense the anxiety of the parents watching and that became a distraction and led to the kids also feeling the anxiety, which diminished their success rate.

Eventually, I rigged the system. I didn't allow the parents to watch on the first day, and I used a "ringer" who was the son of one of our staff members. He was only about six years old but was comfortable in the gear and had repeated success. So, I always had him go first.

The other kids saw him comfortably scuba diving and the success rate went up because they saw that he had no fear. There was really nothing to fear because they were always in my control and never dove more than three feet below the surface.

The kids learned that to overcome fear, they needed to trust that I would not let anything bad happen to them. And they needed to trust themselves that nothing bad could happen if they just went along with the guidance I provided.

I also learned more about fear when I was teaching adults scuba diving.

Often, I would be teaching a class, and they would be nodding their heads in agreement with everything I was saying. I would ask if they understood and they would confirm. Then, after we were underwater, I would signal to them to repeat the exercise we had successfully completed on the surface. Surprisingly they would often respond with confusion about what to do, even though they had successfully done it several times on the surface.

Eventually I learned that they had not absorbed the information on the surface because they were so caught up in fear of what would happen underwater that they completely forgot what to do.

Fear is a strong emotion. It blocks logical thinking.

Fear is used in religion and politics. It is divisive. It can inspire hatred.

"Give yourself to our God and our religion or you will never have salvation and will be damned to hell."

"Voting for me or my opponent will ruin our country/state/city."

Fear blocks love. For if you are afraid to trust, you can never have authentic love.

Overcoming fear allows you to experience confidence in

yourself to realize that anything is possible if you are willing to commit yourself to the goal and do the necessary work.

Challenge Questions:

How does fear impact how you live your life?

Does fear of failure stop you from trying new things?

How can you overcome fear in your life?

What would the existentialists say?

Deep Dive

WHAT IF WHAT WE FEAR MOST—OUR DARKNESS, OUR SHADOWS—HOLDS THE KEYS TO OUR FREEDOM?
—TASH PERICIC

We all have a dark side, a shadow self; painful memories and childhood trauma we want to leave buried, traits we aren't proud of, regrets and mistakes we'd rather hide from. We tell ourselves that these parts aren't "really me" and with those words, we sever these aspects from ourselves and become fractured. This denial of our shadow creates a constant conflict between who we are and who we want to be, or more—who we are capable of being, our truth.

We have been conditioned to fear the shadow side of ourselves. As kids, we were told to smile and be happy; being angry, sad, resentful, jealous wasn't ok. We were taught to push these emotions down, not to express them, that it was bad or wrong to show these things. When really, we should have been taught to be curious about these emotions, but instead fear was instilled. We internalized these messages and so began the process of becoming and remaining fractured.

As adults, we carry these lessons with us and learn new ways to cope—we deny, hide, numb, repress… but no matter how hard we try, our shadow remains. It seems the more we deny it, the more it bursts forth to the surface, disconnecting us from our truth, fracturing us further.

"The sad truth is that running from our shadow only intensifies its power. Denying it only leads to more pain, suffering, regret and resignation. If we fail to take responsibility and extract the wisdom that has been hidden beneath the surface of our conscious minds, the shadow will take charge and instead of us being able to have control over it, the shadow winds up having control over us, triggering the shadow effect. Our dark side then starts making our decisions for us, stripping us of our right to make conscious choices whether it's what food we will eat, how much we will spend or what addiction we will succumb to. Our shadow incites us to act out in ways we never imagined we could and to waste vital energy on bad habits and repetitive behavior."

—Debbie Ford, *The Shadow Effect*

When we are living unconsciously, more often than not, we don't realize we are numbing, hiding, or repressing. Yet, we feel it. Something whispers, "You are better than this, life can be more beautiful than this…" I don't know about anyone else, but this used to upset me even more, because I knew I was capable of being better but I didn't know how to reconcile the difference. I felt broken, like something was deeply wrong with me. Turning to my pain felt like it would destroy me. Little did I know that not turning to it was destroying me.

About five years ago, I had my "dark night of the soul," where I came face-to-face with my shadows. I had moved to Croatia and married my love; I should've been over the moon but instead I was drowning in depression. It was the first time I was truly still in my life; no work, friends, family, social life, not even the language… there was nothing to define or distract me, just me. I was also with a man who really saw me, which was as beautiful as it was confronting.

There I was, stripped bare, standing naked in the spotlight of love, exposed, with nowhere to hide.

Stand and face it or turn and run away?

Everything was being forced to the surface, but for the first time in my life, I didn't want to run. I had found my soulmate and I didn't want to lose him. I intuited that I had no choice but to stand and face my shadows or risk losing it all.

A montage of all of the ways I had been hurt and all the ways I had hurt others, flashed before my eyes. I was forced to bear witness to much of my pain. This was my rock bottom. I was already deeply depressed and this cracked me wide open. After months of tears and fighting, when my soul felt utterly spent and exhausted, somewhere from my depths, a pained voice roared, "I don't like myself!"

There it was, the truth I feared.

When I stood and looked at all my pain, when I faced my shadow self, I didn't like what I saw. This was a rude awakening—realizing you don't like yourself is enough to wake you to yourself. And my fear that turning toward my pain would destroy me, was founded—it did destroy me, just not in the way I imagined. It burned to the ground the false image I had of myself and what remained was raw truth—a flawed, imperfect human.

And there, drenched in sweat and tears, surrounded by my shadows and the acceptance that I was flawed, human; I found something unexpected—a hint of freedom and whisperings of grace.

One of the most painful truths I had to face was based around my issues with alcohol. My shadows held pain from childhood that I'd never acknowledged—abandonment issues from a mother who left us and anger toward the alcoholic and abusive stepmother who raised us. I didn't understand that this was the source of a lot of my pain because I refused to look. Alcohol became my means of numbing and escaping; it started off fun and harmless, but over time, alcohol caused me more pain— the cure became the cause.

I would get black-out drunk regularly, and on those nights, I would do and say things I could never imagine. The happy, confident, kind, compassionate person—the aspects I associated as the "real me"—would disappear and someone I didn't recognise would take her place. Spraying abusive words

Deep Dive

at people I loved, hurting myself physically and emotionally. Reaching for alcohol was almost an unconscious act, just like reaching for food or resorting to violence—these are simply well-worn paths we walk to displace the pain. When you repeat actions long enough, they become unconscious habits.

"Everyone carries a shadow, and the less it is embodied in the individual's conscious life, the blacker and denser it is."

—Carl Jung

Every time I was told what I did (I rarely remembered), I would feel deep shame, which reinforced my inner dialogue that I was unworthy of love, a horrible person. It cut me deep to hear these things when I knew that I was capable of so much more. Feeling the divide between who I was (my actions) and who I knew I was capable of being (my truth) was beyond painful. I couldn't face it. I didn't realize my refusal to acknowledge these aspects was the thing that was keeping me shackled, keeping me locked in these negative cycles and patterns of behavior. Downward spiralling became my normal trajectory.

We can't change something we refuse to acknowledge.

The night I came face-to-face with my shadows, the whisperings of grace and compassion I found told me that the only way I was going to survive (myself) and become who I knew I was capable of being, was to turn toward my shadows and make peace with them. From that moment, I made a vow to lean into the discomfort of facing my shadows. Every time something came up, every time I was triggered, I turned toward the source and tried to practice curiosity—What are you trying to teach?

Alongside acceptance (judgment is just another ego trap that keeps us bound so we can't move forward) —"I recognise you, I see you, it's ok."

It was a slow, hard slog at the beginning but eventually it got easier. It really does get easier. I have come to see that living with shame and being ruled by my shadows was far more painful than facing them.

The more we accept our pain and flaws, the more we become whole, our best and truest version.

Facing our shadows isn't just about the obvious and dramatic experiences either—like our drunk alter ego. Nor do we need to hit rock bottom before we face them. Every day we are offered the opportunity to accept ourselves. Every time we act out or witness flashes of anger, jealousy, resentment, rage; any time we are lazy, selfish, unkind or act in ways we don't consider to be our "true nature"—We are offered a chance to acknowledge that these things exist in us.

When we practice acceptance (instead of judgement, denial, or repression), with each offer of acceptance, we welcome a piece of us home. Every time we acknowledge and accept the truth, we choose to live more consciously instead of through limiting self-beliefs, fears, and learned behaviors (our shadows).

Until we accept all of who we are, no matter how hard we try, our shadows will continue to sabotage us, they will block us from getting to the highest expression of our truth.

This doesn't mean that we never get angry, jealous, or feel any sort of pain—this is all part of the normal human experience. So, the goal isn't to remove these things from our life but to deal with them in a better way. When we acknowledge our shadows, we get to choose how we respond instead of our shadows choosing for us.

"Carl Jung called it a 'sparring partner.' It is the opponent within us that exposes our flaws and sharpens our skills. It is the teacher, the trainer, and the guide that supports us in uncovering our true magnificence. The shadow is not a problem to be solved or an enemy to be conquered but a fertile field to be cultivated. When we dig our hands into its rich soil, we will discover the potent seeds of the people we most desire to be."
—Debbie Ford, *The Shadow Effect*

This practice has radically transformed my life. Through shadow work and acceptance, I have healed deep wounds, and my relationship with myself and others has improved. I am living more in alignment with my values and truth, not despite my shadows but because of them. In fact, I am in a place where I am grateful for my shadows because they have become my greatest teachers and all of these painful experiences have given me a well of compassion to draw from for others.

Shadow work is never done; it is a constant relationship. I continue to learn and dig deeper, uncovering more false beliefs and wounds that need healing. But I feel more in control and my shadows blind-side me less often than they used to.

I am awake.

Now when I look back, I don't look back with shame and regret; instead I look back with compassion because I see someone living with so much unnecessary pain and struggle. All that time, the shadows I feared would destroy me, actually held the keys to my freedom.

Everything in life exists in duality, we can only know our light, once we know and accept our dark.

"One does not become enlightened by imaging figures of light but by making the darkness conscious."

—Carl Jung

Shadows make us whole, so it is time to welcome them home. The person we wish to be and the life we dream of is waiting.

Challenge Questions:

Have you faced your fears? What are they?

Do you agree with her statement about duality?

Are you familiar with your dark side?

Are you hiding anything from yourself?

Would the existentialists say that you need to face the shadow?

Tash Pericic. I was born in Aotearoa, New Zealand, and am now living in Croatia with my Croatian husband. From as young as I can remember, writing has always been my saviour, my sanctuary, a safe place to express myself, to feel all the feels and even uncover some truths without fear of judgement.

As I began to publish some of these musings, fear of judgement and shame crept in, but I discovered something stronger than these—connection. The more I published my raw truths and experiences, the more I seemed to hit a nerve with others and messages of support and "Thank God, it's not just me" flooded in.

I have always loved writing, now I have realized that conversation and storytelling may be the key to healing and connection; that we are all just messy, complicated, awkward humans, simply trying to do our best.

So, my writing is a way of shining a light in the dark for myself and if it helps light the way for others, even better.

The author and his family

Deep Dive

PART 3
SOCIETY
HUMANKIND

PART 3: SOCIETY/HUMANKIND

In this section we will move outside of the self. We start with family and then explore some of the universal things that relate to issues in our culture/society and humankind. We also explore some fundamentally divisive existential issues in our culture like politics, racism, wealth inequality, and guns.

FAMILY
—DAN BEEMAN

Family is defined as a specific group of people that may be made up of partners, children, parents, aunts, uncles, cousins, and grandparents. An example of a family is a set of parents living with their children. The definition of family is the group of people who share common ancestors.

"In family life, love is the oil that eases friction, the cement that binds closer together, and the music that brings harmony."
—Friedrich Nietzsche

There are many different types of families and family units. Almost all of us have a family of some sort—be it a group of friends, a soul family of people with similar life experiences, a sports team, or a spiritual commonality. You may define your family differently. In this essay, we will explore various familial relationships.

This essay is the most difficult to write, because it is very personal. I referenced my biological family in my personal biography. My siblings have all achieved a great deal of success in their lives. All are married with loving families and financial success. As I have said, our parents taught us to pursue our dreams. And, with work, our dreams, no matter what, can be achieved.

The upside of that teaching is that each sibling has done that in their own, unique way. The downside is that it led to a geographical dispersal of seven siblings across the United States and the world—each pursuing their own destiny. Even in the age of social media, physical separation can lead to emotional separation.

With social media, distance gives a certain safety net for judgement of others. People (siblings) can take snippets of information from a social media post and leap to a judgement based on the limited perspective of the information they receive. Then, they subjectively process that information from their unique lens.

As discussed previously, greatness and success are both subjective. Those who have achieved some form of success according to the society (or family) often project their idea of success on others, which helps reinforce their idea of success. This becomes self-perpetuating and reinforces the bond between the people who have similar existence.

Others, whose journey in life takes a different path from the "accepted" reinforced way, get judged because it is different

Deep Dive

from the person who is doing the judging. Endorsing or accepting the different path would then jeopardize their chosen path, and, therefore would delegitimize their chosen path of success.

This is where it becomes personal for me. I have not followed a traditional path in my life and have made some unconventional decisions: my enlistment in the army, leaving a job raising money for the MS Society, working for Club Med as an Activities Director, etc.

Superficially, it appeared that I left a "good" job doing good things for others for a life of hedonistic pursuits. The truth is that in Club Med I grew as a person more than I did at any other job in my life. It paid almost nothing but enabled me to discover and develop skills that I had never known. It challenged me to be proactive with interactions, and live more fully by trying new things and understanding different cultures.

Prior to marriage, my life/career decisions almost never involved pursuit of material success but instead quality of life.

I have also taken jobs in other states and countries away from my family. This has been perceived as running away from responsibility when it was actually the opposite—accepting and taking responsibility. In those cases, I took the best-paying job to support my family. Being away was a sacrifice for me but benefitted my family because they were able to come visit and experience a new culture as a result of these jobs. Most recently, I rented my condo in Palm Desert for the month of March 2020. I chose to go to Playa Del Carmen, MX, to launch my

Pickleball Consulting business—helping resorts implement pickleball programs to enhance their revenue streams. Once there, the pandemic began. Instead of returning to the U.S., where it was more dangerous, I chose to stay in a remote spot to socially distance while writing most of this book. It was one of the best decisions of my life! It also opened me up to judgement by others.

This has led siblings to refer to my decisions and actions in life according to the Sinatra song—doing it my way.

The more I felt questioned by them, the more I felt isolated from them. This led to me questioning my intuitive life decisions, but it also helped me reflect on what is important to me.

Those reflections, my personal deep dive, resulted in what you are reading now.

My relationship with some of my siblings and my daughter is, to put it politely, strained. With my daughter, I am frustrated because I see her making mistakes that don't need to be made with her life. I see her making the same mistakes I made. As her parent, I want her to have a path that is not so difficult. But I see that she needs to follow her path as I followed mine.

I feel successful in that I have manifested my own destiny. My life is filled with many varied, exotic experiences. I have created more memories than many people have in a lifetime. I wouldn't trade them for all the material wealth in the world.

With some siblings, I sense they don't understand my path,

which is so different from theirs. They have achieved great success. I try not to judge others, but for some, judgement is an organic lens.

So, then, what is success?

In a subjective and capitalistic society, success is often calculated in material and monetary ways. It is perpetuated like a stone tossed into a body of water, causing an outward ripple. The richest and most "successful" are at the center—They are admired by those outside of the first circle and that continues as the circle widens.

While biology has created a connection between siblings, parents, and their children, our environment, belief systems, and experiences can impact our opinions of others who share the same DNA.

As we get older, many of us regenerate and create our own families. As parents, we try to build our families and teach our children according to our values. And this cycle continues.

As we age and often become parents, our judgement lens is magnified. We judge our kids' behavior and try to modify it when it does not align with our belief system. It becomes difficult to change this judgement lens because our subjective lens wants to reinforce our way of thinking and living. This, too, is self-perpetuating.

So, many of us are simultaneously parents and children. It is that dynamic in our existence with our ever-changing experiences that makes our relationships ever-evolving. Your family, however you define it, should be filled with love.

One example of non-judgmental love comes from the siblings of my mother. They came from alcoholic, divorced parents. There were five kids who superficially were very different. It would have been so easy for them to judge each other and be divided. But instead, they overcame the adversity of their childhood, banded together, and became lifelong friends who supported and loved each other deeply—without judgement.

Dan Beeman with his family.

Deep Dive

Challenge Questions:

How do you define family?

What does your family look like to you?

Do you have several different families?

Do you find yourself judging or judged?

How does that feel?

PARENTING
—DAN BEEMAN

Parenting or child rearing is the process of promoting and supporting the physical, emotional, social, and intellectual development of a child from infancy to adulthood. Parenting refers to the intricacies of raising a child and not exclusively to a biological relationship.

Parenting styles vary by historical time period, race/ethnicity, social class, and other social features. Additionally, research supports that parental history both in terms of attachments of varying quality as well as parental psychopathology, particularly in the wake of adverse experiences, can strongly influence parental sensitivity and child outcomes.

"We may not be able to prepare the future for our children, but we can at least prepare our children for the future."
—Franklin Roosevelt

My wife and I met when we were 36. Neither of us had been

married or had kids. I fell for her stunning beauty immediately and I pursued her with relentless passion. I asked her to move in with me just a couple of months after we met. I proposed to her the day we moved in together, and we were married six months later. Our daughter arrived nine months later, and fifteen months after that, we had a son. Days after my son was born, we moved from California to Virginia.

My wife and I could not agree on parenting, and it was what broke up our marriage. She had her way of doing things and I had mine, and they did not coalesce. We were both stuck on being right. We each thought we had the best solution to the inevitable challenges that would occur between two people who were used to doing things their way and were married within a year of meeting each other. And because we sent mixed messages to our kids, they exploited it.

The power dynamics played a big role. For the first five years, I was the provider. My wife was a stay-at-home mom. I made good money and was proud of the nice things our family enjoyed.

I also only knew how my parents parented, with a clean division of labor. My mom oversaw seven kids, and the home was her domain. She cooked, cleaned, shopped, taught, supervised, refereed, read, pleaded, drove, drove, and drove in more ways than one.

My father was an exemplary provider and enjoyed his role. He was also active in supporting our after-school activities and sports.

This what we followed at first in our marriage, but things changed.

I remember one time when we were living in Virginia with our two babies, I became upset with my wife because she refused to iron my shirts for work. I didn't understand this because my mom always ironed my dad's shirts, even though she was raising seven kids. My wife didn't appreciate the comparison. In retrospect, we could easily have afforded dry cleaning.

After two years in Virginia, we moved back to California for my new job. It was a good-paying job, and they also paid for our move. In 2007, we bought and renovated our home without any concern of costs. I was laid off from my job just months after that, and then a big recession hit at the same time. Times got tough. My wife had to get a job. I lost my mojo. Our roles changed. The power dynamics changed. I became the stay-at-home parent. I was jealous and resentful. I felt marginalized.

This was the case for the next twelve years. It led to many problems at home. Eventually, our marriage dissolved.

At the end, we had all the superficial representations of success and happiness—a beautiful house, with beautiful kids, a couple of dogs, in a great neighborhood in the school district our kids wanted and near all their friends. We had a pool in the back yard and, on paper, a wonderful life. Yet underneath, the power dynamics torpedoed our marriage.

My wife, the breadwinner, was a very hard-working woman. She was proud of supporting her family and willing to do whatever was necessary to pay the bills. Sometimes, this was at the expense of time with me and the kids. I was resentful.

I was supposed to oversee the home. Frankly, I wasn't very good at it. I could make a decent breakfast, make sandwiches, and grilled a mean steak, but was not adept with other cooking or cleaning.

My wife loved pets. But, remember, she worked full-time. It started with a cat. Then another cat, then a dog. Then another dog. All against my wishes. She loved animals. I needed to adjust. Instead, I became more resentful.

Beginning in eighth grade, our beautiful, smart, talented daughter began to have problems at school with rules, authority, grades, and friends. It was highly disturbing for me because I knew her talent and capabilities. I met with the counselors to seek solutions, but it only got worse. Finally, we had a meeting—both parents, several teachers, a counselor, and the principal.

It was a nightmare. My wife blamed the school officials and seemingly refused to hold our daughter accountable. I became upset that none of the responsibility of the behavior was attributed to our daughter by my wife. The power divide between my wife and I was on full display for all to witness. Eventually, both our daughter and my wife walked out of the meeting. My wife went back to work. Nothing was resolved.

This was the beginning of the end, and it only got worse from there. We both went to our areas of comfort: My wife believes in unconditional love. I believe kids need to learn accountability.

This is the gulf that our kids exploited.

It really takes both unconditional love and accountability. It is possible to do both at the same time. Kids need both parents and both perspectives. But when parents are stubborn and stuck on being right, problems will ensue.

Challenge Questions:

How do you parent?

How do you resolve disagreements with your spouse? Are you stuck on being right?

Is it better to have an unhappy marriage or stay together for the kids?

Which is more important for kids to learn: unconditional love or accountability?

What would the existentialists say?

The author with his children.

Dick and Dan Beeman

FROM PARENT TO CHILD TO PARENT AND CHILD: MUSINGS FROM DAN'S FATHER —DICK BEEMAN

In rereading your articulate invitation to take the deep dive with you, I appreciate your knowledge and candid dialogue with yourself.

You, calling us your audience, to "never stop exploring yourself!"

Quoting key philosophers and wisdom teachers encourages us to "become the person you really are, by way of honest introspection!"

Deep Dive

Dan, that is you and me together absorbed on our adventures together at Spirit Rock...and Harbin Hot Springs.

Who do you want to be, is a daily mantra for both of us, calling each other!

Your authentic recollections and life stories reveal your life process.

Thank you for sharing.

May I offer a few loving insights?

The path leading from the false self-serving to the True Self, is paved with evolving self-awareness, and the willingness to change.

"Who am I?" Jean Val Jean cried out in the unforgettable theme lyric of *Les Miserable*. His is a gripping story of personal transformation!

Your sincere challenge for us is to fathom our individual faults and failings, while recognizing the goodness and Godness within. This our core destiny!

"Broken but being made Whole."

The honesty in your personal biography, wherein you identify yourself as hedonistic, in a failed marriage, and an absentee father was direct but not final.

It need not be written in stone...

Yearning about who you want to be is the deep drive while writing your book.

(Talk to me about personal transformation.)

Dan, examine your creative communication skills, so effectively demonstrated in your "Buddy Comedy" film script, and the *Deep Dive* book manuscript, as well as your academic essay!

Very impressive.

Reality check. When you recently found your daughter "not speaking to me," did it occur to you that your precious daughter might be aching for a close personal relationship with her dad?

Life is all about relationships, Dan...awareness of self...and other's needs.

This sounds like your challenge to all of us in *Deep Dive*.

What else to offer...

Leaving Callie a white board list of directions doesn't hold a candle to your in-person attention and gentle conversation.

She needs you....She is not in the military.

Your patient, thoughtful availability in person is life-giving and crucial to your beautiful children and their mother, all of whom crave your attention.

You and I jointly propose to honestly self cultivate, meaning to notice, admit, and transform our shortcomings.

Maslow preaches Self Actualization as high in his hierarchy of needs, but that dream includes and requires a discipline of primary needs.

You are a traveler and seeker—Mexico, Belize, Panama, Playa del Carmen, Palm Desert, and Tahoe. These are all tempting escapes.

We all covet Playa del Carmen. What else calls…?

Love always,
Father

LIFE
—SEAN CLEARY

"It's better to burn out than to fade away."

—Neil Young

You can't have death without life, so let's start there. Life: What is it and what it is!

Life is all about living and more about giving. My spiritual mentor and Aunt, Sister Ellen Carroll, worked tirelessly for years at Visitation, a South-side Chicago Catholic Elementary School. Sister Ellen, or "E" as our family referred to her, embodied the concept of giving like few people I have ever met.

"E" was selfless in giving of herself to others and truly lived by the motto "the gift you have received give as a gift" paraphrased from a Catholic translation of Matthew 10:8. "E" backed up her

Deep Dive

words with action when she initiated the Visitation Scholarship Program in 1989. This program assisted in providing parochial education to at-risk elementary schoolchildren for the purpose of being a segue to private high schools.

This was vitally important for "E" to create an opportunity for inner-city kids to break the cycle of poverty through a more advanced education. "E" realized you could only get into college if you graduated from high school. But she also knew you needed to first graduate from a grade school, especially one that emphasized core values of discipline, respectfulness, and gratitude.

"E" saw an immediate need for a structured program, and her passion and persistence helped transform the lives of hundreds of marginalized young people and their families. How resilient was "E"? Even as she battled terminal cancer in 2005, Visitation associates would roll her wheelchair, while she was connected to an IV and chemotherapy machines, into the hospital lobby so she could continue working on her mission in life.

"E" was a Sister Act long before Whoopi Goldberg famously played "a nun who could have fun." She lived life joyfully and abundantly and was especially proud of her deep Irish roots, and cherished a couple of trips to the Emerald Isle. "E" was a jubilant spirit who wasn't afraid to—and in fact loved to—dance and sing. Her favorite songs were "Celebration" by Kool and the Gang and "We Are Family" by Sister Sledge. Both of these tunes were always on the play list at our large family wedding gatherings.

"E" would boldly sing and dance to these anthems along with the rest of us. These two musical selections epitomized exactly what "E" stood for: celebrating every single day of life and standing together as a family. These were both critically important ideals in her life.

"E" exhibited her love of and leadership for her family in many ways, including regular communication with her siblings, my cousins, and myself. This included her randomly mailing us challenging reading assignments, such as *The Earth Speaks* by Steve Van Matre and "Nuevo Catholics" by David Rieff. Reading these materials was a strongly suggested expectation of our teacher and mentor, "E." These heady snippets would often lead to dialogue and debate regarding some of the key issues of the day, including taking proper care of our planet or the acceptance of immigrant Catholics.

"E" dancing

In my case, "E's" love of Earth inspired me to devote time to picking up trash in our community and to become obsessed with recycling. "E" used to say that if we choose to ignore or accept something like litter on the sidewalks, it could potentially develop into other more serious neighborhood and societal problems. This came from good authority, as "E" served the poorest of the poor in Chicago's Back of the Yards neighborhoods. "E" witnessed first-hand the adverse effects of malaise and complacency and fought fiercely to counteract it. "E" was absolutely colorblind and instilled and expected acceptance and tolerance of others from us, her family, as well. Her openness to others has affected and benefitted me over the years.

Growing up in a 100% Caucasian community in Columbus, Ohio, I had limited, if any, opportunity to embrace ethnicity. That fortunately changed when I enrolled as an older student at Ohio University (OU) in Athens. I was a non-traditional student who worked in the summer and fall so I could pay for and attend winter and spring quarters. To me, attending OU was like living in the United Nations, as I was exposed and introduced to a whole new set of friends from Iran, Libya, Malaysia, and Norway, among other countries.

"E" always believed that if we only associated with a select type or group of people, we would be limiting our breadth and depth of life experiences. This was brilliant and welcome advice that has led to several meaningful lifelong friendships for me. I recently reconnected with Dr. Imtiaz Hussein, who now oversees a global studies program at a University in Bangladesh. One of the wisest and most delightful people I've ever met,

Imtiaz, several others, and myself routinely gathered in an OU cafeteria to discuss the hot topics of the day. These table talks provided me with a more expansive collegiate learning experience that I cherish to this day.

Indeed, "E" led by example, accepting, loving, and coveting friendships with all walks of life—friends who were every bit as devoted to her as she was to them. Her Sister motherhouse was in pastoral Sinsinawa, Wisconsin, the home of Mound bread. If you don't know about Mound bread, sorry for your bad luck! These weighty loaves of cinnamon bread deliciousness were homemade by the good sisters in a mammoth kitchen there. It is most appropriate that the breaking and sharing of Mound bread was "E's" calling card, and a traditional Christmas treat for her family and friends.

"E" was much beloved by our family and anybody who had the pleasure of meeting her—and continues to serve as my spiritual mentor fifteen years after her death.

Why? Because she managed to make God enjoyable and fun for me and many others.

How did she do that? In many ways, including music, psalms, nature, and poems like Rudyard Kipling's "If." She gave "If" to me for my high school graduation gift, and I still try to abide by it to this day.

In the quiet of the woods, I can still hear "E's" resounding roars of laughter with my mom and three other siblings. We affectionately referred to them as the "Iron Five" for their closeness and love of each other.

Good humor aside, "E" was emphatic and non-compromising, and principled without fault. As an example, when it came to attending church, she accepted absolutely no excuses for not being in the pew. Yes, her faith in God clearly played a major role in her life and drove her insatiable and selfless desire to help the less fortunate.

"E," my friends, lived!

I have also had the privilege of working with older adults in nursing facilities for the past forty years. I have witnessed many residents, even well into their hundreds, who still exhibit youthful exuberance and an appetite for personal development. They have learned the secret to life, which is much about attitude and growth.

"E" at a family graduation

One of these residents, Jean, used to say she was "plenty-nine" and remained joyful despite having experienced difficult losses over the course of her life, including the love of her life, her husband of over 60 years. She longed for him every day and showed me love letters he'd crafted and mailed to her when he was overseas, serving as a soldier in World War I.

These letters were inscribed with such artistry, care, and beauty that they could have found a place in a museum's archives. I remember the radiant look on Jean's face as she reminisced about the love she shared with her husband. What kept her going was more than her fond memories of the love of her life, however.

She was also an accomplished English grade-school teacher, who was largely responsible for literacy in a sizable community in Ohio. How do I know that? It became increasingly evident of the mark she made, as scores of former students stopped by to visit with her routinely. Jean was, as Fred Rogers used to say, "a helper," and was always looking for ways to help others, specifically her students, who she helped develop into doctors, nurses, business people, politicians, teachers, musicians, and professional athletes, among other occupations—and they invariably attributed their successes to this teacher.

Jean also helped former Ohio State football coach Woody Hayes with his writing and was his frequent proofreader. Though macular degeneration had robbed her of her sight, Jean feverishly listened to talking books "that stretched her" and Ohio State sports on the radio.

In other words, she kept on living until the day she passed away at age 105. When I asked her how she lived so long, she replied, "I kept breathing!"

Jean's favorite saying, that I recite by heart to this day, was: "Good, better, best. Never let it rest, until you make your good better, and your better best!"

Jean was always trying to do her best and spent a lifetime bringing out the best in others she taught and befriended over the years. Jean was easy to admire and hard not to like. She didn't feel sorry for herself and maintained a positive outlook on life despite having some major setbacks. Experience is indeed a great teacher.

Jean often referred to herself as a bad penny. She was really more of a precious coin!

These are two examples of people I admire and respect for how they embraced life, despite being confronted with a terminal illness and advanced age, respectively.

It is incredibly powerful and meaningful to honor those we can still make contact with and those who have passed before us.

Challenge Questions:

Take a few minutes to acknowledge someone who has positively affected you by the way they have lived and what gift you received from them. If your impactful person(s) is still alive, how meaningful would it be for them to hear from you at this time?

If they are no longer with us, could you reach out to one of their family members and relay your thoughts and feelings to them?

Imagine their surprise and delight in hearing about someone they love being memorialized by you.

DEATH
—SEAN CLEARY

Speaking of death, I have been dubbed a "crasher" for attending so many funerals over the years. Working in nursing facilities, death is a too frequent occupational hazard. Perhaps because I've attended a host of wakes, viewings, and the like, I believe I have a pretty healthy understanding and perspective on death.

Despite the number of funerals I've had the privilege of being involved with, I don't consider myself de-sensitized to the process. I'm appreciative of lives often long and well lived, and in the Irish tradition, can cry and laugh at the same time at funerals.

My mom taught our family to have fun with the post-death process; she once sent my uncle a cemetery postcard, writing "Wish you were here," and mailed it to him. The apple didn't fall far from the tombstone as my brother Tim wrote on our grandpa's 80th birthday card, "Well, Grandpa, goes to show you only the good die young."

Our family came by an acceptance of death honestly. Mom was referred to as the honorary "cemeterian" by family members for her frequency of trips to multiple cemeteries in Columbus, Ohio. She was meticulous in her care of the gardening she provided around the gravestones. She taught us to honor those we loved and missed, specifically her deceased grandparents, who helped raise her, her parents, and my brother Kevin, who ultimately died after being involved in a serious auto accident in May 1983.

Kevin's death remains one of the most impactful losses of my life.

Initially after his accident, Kevin was hospitalized in a coma in the intensive care unit at the Ohio State University Hospital. He eventually was transferred to a head trauma unit at Good Samaritan Hospital in Zanesville, Ohio.

Kevin received terrific care there for over two years, including extensive therapy services and a two-week trial in a hyperbaric oxygen chamber. All the while, our parents never gave up hope and prayed faithfully for a miracle recovery.

Our family and Kevin's fiancée took many trips to Eastern Ohio to love and support him, but it just wasn't meant to be; Kevin never emerged from the coma and appropriately died just before Thanksgiving in 1985. I was truly grateful that his life came to a merciful end. Why? He was largely bedridden for two and a half years and "existing" was not the life Kevin ever would have envisioned—or wanted—for himself.

He was always a guy who lived life to the extreme, with great gusto and a sense of urgency. Prior to his accident, it's as though he had a premonition that his time on Earth was limited; and so he was more of a sprinter than a marathoner.

As examples, he was a voracious traveler and a student who never stopped learning. Kevin was highly curious and prided himself on his vocabulary, which he honed with a new word daily, and he would attempt to sneak obscure words into everyday conversation. He was intense and highly competitive, which falls to reason being the de facto leader of seven boys.

In case you can't detect, Kevin was my idol and mentor in every way. I repeatedly followed his lead and he seldom, if ever, steered me wrong. He was truly a trendsetter and a Renaissance man;

Deep Dive

as examples, he was making his own beer ("Golden Bogie" and "Bogie Bock," both largely undrinkable) back in the mid 70's. He also served as our rogue white-water rafting guide on untamed West Virginia and Pennsylvania rivers. He was my backyard coach and heavily influenced my athletic endeavors as well. I essentially mimicked Kevin's European backpacking trip, college selections, theatrical pursuits, musical tastes, and infatuation with the Baltimore Colts.

In retrospect, I believe the reason I emulated him was because Kevin treated me as an equal and not as a punky younger brother. For instance, he welcomed me to move in with him and two of his peers when I was a ripe 19-year-old. That was a really big deal to me at the time—I was four years junior to my older brother and his 23-year-old roommates—and yet Kevin thought I was worthy!

More than that, he was compassionate beyond belief. Our oldest brother Rick was unfortunately diagnosed with schizophrenia at the age of eighteen. Kevin, just a year younger than Rick, took on the role of doing his very best to try and normalize Rick's life with camping and concert trips, encouraging his guitar playing and distance running, among other things.

Kevin never stopped trying to engage Rick, and his love, care, and interest were not lost on me or our family. He was a savior to our parents, and we all responded to his deep, bellowed voice and laugh. These are just a few of the reasons I worshipped my brother and readily followed his lead.

Even after his death, I still celebrate Kevin's life. I believe strongly in serendipity, as did my mom, who didn't just write off odd occurrences as coincidences. She always encouraged us to pay attention to the everyday occurrences of life and that if we really did, miracles would abound.

One such moment occurred while I attended my daughter Annie's grade school soccer game in 2005. At the game, I noticed a mother I knew from the local library standing by herself, watching the action. Her daughter was playing for the opposing team, but nonetheless I started talking with this rival mom—a rarity for a competitor. She knew that I worked in healthcare, and I knew she had home-schooled her children. I asked her if she had worked outside of the home and she mentioned that she was a physical therapist who had worked in acute care settings. I asked her where she worked and she said Good Samaritan Hospital in Zanesville. I asked her when and where she worked there and she replied, "The head trauma unit from 1983–1985."

Bells went off in my head! I asked her if she remembered my brother, Kevin Cleary, who was also there at that time. She asked me what he did there, and I told her he was a head trauma patient. She became exasperated, and said, "Kevin?! I worked with him every day for two years. I remember your parents well—they were there all the time. They were remarkable people and were so appreciative and kind."

I became incredibly emotional over this discovery and cried. I thanked her for being there to take care of my brother. I had never had the privilege of meeting this caregiver as I usually visited Kevin in the evenings and on weekends. I called my parents on my way home from Annie's game to share this story of serendipity with them.

Annie asked me why I was crying as I spoke with my mom and dad. I told her it was news about her deceased uncle who she never had a chance to meet—but who had just let me know he was okay. Not coincidentally this encounter occurred on Kevin's birthday, August 28, 2005.

When I think of death, it's hard for me not to think of eulogies. Morbidly perhaps, I enjoy paying tribute to people who have died, and I try my best to capture the essence of them in eulogies. I hope it's better than having the randomly assigned minister standing before the grief-stricken, announcing, "Well I never knew Charlie, but I heard he was an okay person." Not exactly the greatest, most meaningful send-off. And when it comes to the dash on the grave marker, let's have that signify something—like hopefully a life well lived.

I have been honored to deliver eulogies for my brother Kevin, my dad, my father-in-law Bob Kirwin, and my best friend, among others. In each of their deaths, we celebrated their lives again.

I was one of seven sons of my dad, G.R. Cleary. Some might think it's unusual to call dad by his initials, but then again, our relationship with G.R. was highly unusual. He was the best dad I could have ever hoped for, as he was also our best friend and biggest fan.

G.R. loved adventure and was the proud owner of a StarCraft

sailboat and a dated outboard. Safe to say we didn't belong to any yacht clubs, but we sure had fun, and sometimes we even managed to get the boats on the water. Unfortunately, we made Gilligan look like St. Brendan the Navigator!

We managed to lose a mast on the sailboat and once Dad hauled our outboard eight hours to a Northern Michigan lake, only for it not to start. Regardless, he had a joyful countenance about him, was humble as could be, and was the nicest, kindest man I've ever known. I had the honor of being with Dad and Mom when Dad took his last peaceful breath.

Dad wasn't afraid to die, but clearly didn't want to go without Mom, either. His consolation was being reunited with Kevin again, as a part of him and Mom perished along with Kevin. After almost a sixty-year love affair, their being separated by Dad dying was hard to witness.

My father-in-law's last couple of years were very trying for somebody who had been so strong for so long. As Bob's health declined, for him to rely on the kindness of strangers was a role of the strangest order for him. One of Bob's caregivers told me about one of his last nightmares he had shared with her. Bob's nightmare? Not being able to help people anymore.

He was not one to ask for assistance. As an example, I will never forget seeing Bob at a backyard barbecue, with his trembling hand, trying to scoop baked beans onto a plastic fork handle. The fork's plastic prongs had broken and he didn't want to trouble anyone so...he didn't.

We still display the plastic handle on our kitchen mantle as a reminder of his quiet strength and resiliency. It was fitting the night before he died that many of his children gathered around his bedside and prayed the rosary with him. He couldn't have died any happier, as he was surrounded by the love of his family and was reunited with Ruth, his beautiful bride who had passed away just a month before.

What would you do, if you were suddenly diagnosed with a terminal disease and had a week to live?

Is there a family member you were at odds with who you could reach out to?

Are you pleased with it and if not, what's missing from your life?

Fill in the blanks and you are making strides to living a fulfilled life before it's too late.

When I think of death, I think back to the days of my youth, when I was positively horrified by the prospect of dying. I recall being in bed with dark thoughts and feeling very unsettled about it all. I imagined myself laying underground in a casket and that wasn't terribly reassuring to a young boy.

It was hard at times to get those disturbing thoughts out of my head, as I imagined myself no longer being alive, and being underground, to boot. Growing up with a belief that emphasized us to be God-fearing didn't help matters much either. Everything associated with the church of my youth was dark or black—the confessional, for instance, couldn't have been much darker. The cassocks, the shoes, the glasses. Black, black, black—It was a flat-out black attack.

At this stage, I was beyond limbo and was either going to go straight to heaven—or heaven forbid, hell. And it all depended on choices—choices to sin or not. I would go to the confessional routinely but would invariably make up sins because none of us were sinless. We were told that repeatedly by the priests and nuns, even the lay teachers told us that.

So, with my made-up sins I was trying to absolve myself from sin so when I was laying in the casket I would at least have half a chance of getting to heaven. Better there than a casket in the ground.

I can't help but think of the thousands of people who have died during the Covid-19 pandemic and the inability of the deceased to be comforted by loving family members or friends. Equally tragic are the survivors who are missing out on opportunities to pay tribute to lives well lived or to be able to grieve and/or be consoled.

That's a whole lot of sad, unresolved, end-of-life stuff happening as we speak. Comfort and consolation to all of those who have died during this traumatic time, as well as their family members and friends.

Life and death are not about politics, economics, division, and narcissism. Life and death are about love, peace, respect, and acceptance of others. Nothing's the matter with the latter.

Challenge Questions:

Do you ever think of your mortality and what that looks like?

Do you believe in the afterlife? If you don't—So this is it?

Do you have a living will?

Have you written your obituary, and if so, what's missing?

What comforts you or makes you uncomfortable about death?

Sean Cleary is a husband, father, sports fan, and writer who finds humor in everyday existence. He has 40 plus years of experience in the health care industry and focuses on treating people with compassion. He and his wife Rosie live in Ohio and are the proud parents to two caring children.

GUN VIOLENCE IN AMERICA
ESSAY ON GUNS
—DAN BEEMAN

I hate guns. I hate what they represent—one person using the power of a gun to inflict their power of force on another person.

I have a very personal experience when I was in the Army, in which a person used a gun to impose their will upon me to do something I did not want to do. That gun, pointed at me, threatening my life, gave the other person the power over my free will. It changed my life forever. The details are too personal to share, but the impact has stayed with me. I have nightmares about it and am unable to erase it from my mind.

An argument can be made that if I'd had a gun, I could have "neutralized the situation." I could have shot him. But what is the end result of that situation? Someone is still dead. I would have to live with that as well. Killing is not a good thing. Love and compassion are good things.

THE SECOND AMENDMENT

A WELL-REGULATED MILITIA, BEING NECESSARY TO THE SECURITY OF A FREE STATE, THE RIGHT OF THE PEOPLE TO KEEP AND BEAR ARMS, SHALL NOT BE INFRINGED.

What does the Second Amendment mean? This question is at the center of one of the most divisive debates in modern American constitutional law. The amendment, ratified in 1791, itself contains 27 words: "A well-regulated Militia, being necessary to the security of a free State, the right of the people to keep and bear Arms, shall not be infringed."

At that time, a gun was a musket that took on average 20 seconds to fire between rounds or three per minute. Today, legal semi-automatic weapons fire at a rate of **40 rounds per minute.** That is more than every other second!

Magazines today carry more rounds that can be fired in one minute that would take at least 10 minutes when guns were legalized in 1791. At that time, the accuracy, bullet power, firing problems, and lack of magazines made the weapon far more inefficient.

Did the authors and ratifiers of this amendment intend for a society with the biggest police force and military in the world to have citizens with more guns than it has people?

Do you see a problem with this in our society, where there is an average of one mass murder per day in the United States?

Is this not a fundamental existential dilemma in our society?

The author as a young man, in the army.

Deep Dive

Hypothetical Case Study

Almost any adult person can buy a gun in the USA....

A person walks into a store and buys a gun....

A person with a gun randomly kills one or more people....

Thoughts and prayers go out to the victims....

The shooter is vilified....

Editorialists debate causes and solutions....

Two opposing camps evolve:
- Gun control advocates, who blame the availability of guns everywhere in our society, and
- Mental health advocates, who blame the person for being crazy, not the gun.

Gun control advocates lose because there is no legislative support for reasonable solutions....

NRA funds Republicans, who blame mental health deficiencies in people, not the availability and ubiquity of guns in American society....

Anyone with a gun, with no previous mental health issues, can be provoked by someone to set them off in anger on a shooting spree....

Most mass killings with guns are committed by people with no history of mental health problems....

Assuming the shooter is not the product of the environment (set off in anger) suggests that they are mentally flawed, which necessarily means they are genetically flawed, which is caused by a deficiency of their maker....

By natural extension, the same people who blame the mental health issues instead of the gun or the violent environment must be blaming God for producing a fundamentally flawed person who does the shooting....

Therefore, according to this logic, instead of accountability and common-sense solutions to limit guns and save lives, it is somehow God's fault for creating deranged people committing mass murder by using guns in the United States....

It is not the laws that permit semi-automatic weapons and a culture that promotes violence that are responsible for the environment leading to our mass murder epidemic?

Could it be a cultural and legislative issue? Both are corrupted by greed and fueled by money....

But somehow, the blame is laid on something that can't be held accountable or fixed.

How do you hold God accountable or fix God?

Challenge Questions:

Are there too many guns in our culture? If so, why?

Is there responsible legislation that can be enacted to limit guns?

Is the NRA a good organization and doing good things?

Do you have a gun? Why?

What would the existentialists say?

Deep Dive

EXPLORING RACIAL INEQUALITY
—DAN BEEMAN

"One day our descendants will think it incredible that we paid so much attention to things like the amount of melanin in our skin or the shape of our eyes or our gender instead of the unique identities of each of us as complex human beings."
—Franklin Thomas

Racism is bad. But insitituitional racism is much worse. Institituitional racism is woven into the fabric of our society and reinforced through policies and perceptions by those with authority. It is perpetuated by and through themedia using imagery. Institutional Racism is insidious because it does not have the visual imagery that can be easily captured in an image for wide distribution.

One side can show a picture of black people burning down a government vehicle or building and call them looters, thugs, and less than human. The other side can show an image of unnecessary force used by police, armed with weapons and "authority" to keep the peace, beating, smothering, shooting, and killing unarmed people they perceive to be a threat. This imagery is powerful, divisive, and hurtful.

Racism is a trending, troubling, and very relevant topic in our current environment in America. It is much deeper than the Black Lives Matter movement. That movement, which is very powerful and important, is about saving the lives of black people targeted with violence for being black.

Racism is ingrained in the fabric of our culture.

Racism is the festering wound that has undermined the potential harmony among people and the greatness of our democracy in the United States. It exists. It is prevalent. It is exacerbated by ignorance and perpetuated daily through certain cultures.

Either you are racist or are actively acting against racism.

There is no middle ground.

I have personal, relevant experience regarding race. When I served in the U.S. Army from 1982–1984, I learned so much about people from different ethnicities.

I saw first-hand how discrimination exists. As a white man, I had no idea how much I benefitted from my skin color. I had never been a minority before. I was used to being given the benefit of the doubt.

When stationed in Germany, I was housed in a dormitory room with five black men for about a year. Most other rooms in the barracks were semi-segregated—whites, Hispanics, and blacks. I came from a privileged background and had education. This made me different from most of the other enlisted people of my ethnicity. I was kind of a test case to see how I could get along as the only white guy.

In that room, there was no racial hierarchy. In order to get along, we had to respect each other and live in harmony. It meant learning new music, food, and styles of communication.

I embraced this opportunity.

I made new friends and some enemies. Relationships were made not based on skin color but, to quote Martin Luther King, Jr., "on the content of their character." This was liberating and invigorating.

While the military was not a pure meritocracy, it was a place where bullshit did not fly. Most of us were judged on performance as objectively as possible. Anybody who deserved it got promoted—especially on the enlisted side, where all the races were seemingly on an even playing field.

Institutional or systemic racism is embedded as a normal practice within a society or an organization. It can lead to such issues as discrimination in criminal justice, employment, housing, health care, political power, and education.

The term "institutional racism" was first coined in 1967 by Stokely Carmichael and Charles V. Hamilton in *Black Power: The Politics of Liberation*. Carmichael and Hamilton wrote that while individual racism is often identifiable because of its overt nature, institutional racism is less perceptible because of its "less overt, far more subtle" nature. Institutional racism "originates in the operation of established and respected forces in society, and thus receives far less public condemnation than [individual racism]."

Institutional racism was defined by Sir William Macpherson in his "Inquiry into the Matters Arising from the Death of Stephen Lawrence" report (1999) as: "The collective failure of an organization to provide an appropriate and professional service to people because of their color, culture, or ethnic origin. It can be seen or detected in processes, attitudes, and behaviors that amount to discrimination through prejudice, ignorance, thoughtlessness, and racist stereotyping, which disadvantage minority ethnic people."

The origins of America's unjust racial order lie in the most brutal institution of enslavement that human beings have ever concocted. More than 12 million Africans of all ages, shackled in the bottom of ships, were sold into a lifetime of forced labor defined by nonstop violence and strategic dehumanization, all cataloged methodically in sales receipts and ledgers.

Around that "peculiar institution," the thinkers of the time crafted an equally inhumane ideology to justify their brutality, using religious rhetoric in tandem with pseudoscience to rationalize treating humans as chattel. After the Civil War, the arrangements of legal slavery were replaced with those of organized, if not strictly legal, terror. Lynchings, disenfranchisement, and indentured servitude all reinforced racial hierarchy from the period of Reconstruction through Jim Crow segregation and on until the movement for civil rights in the middle of the 20th century.

That's the ugly history most Americans know and acknowledge. But systemic racism also found its way, more insidiously, into the institutions many Americans revere and seek to safe-guard. Established in the 1930s, Social Security helped ensure a stable old age for most Americans, but it initially excluded domestic and agricultural workers, leaving behind two-thirds of black Americans.

Federal mortgage lending programs helped white Americans buy homes after World War II, but black Americans suffered from a shameful Catch-22. Federal policy said that the very presence of a black resident in a neighborhood reduced the value of the homes there, effectively prohibiting African-American residents from borrowing money to buy a home. And sentencing laws of the past several decades meant that poor black Americans were thrown in prison for decades-long terms for consuming one type of cocaine, while their wealthier white counterparts got a slap on the wrist for consuming another.

There's a straight line between these policies and the state of black America today. The lack of Social Security kept black Americans toiling in old age or forced them to the streets. The obstruction of black home ownership, among other factors, has left African Americans poorer and more economically vulnerable, with the average black household worth $17,000 in 2016, while the average white household was worth 10 times that. "Tough on crime" sentencing policies have ballooned the black prison population, torn apart families, and left millions of children to grow up in single-parent homes.

Manifestations of racial inequality

There are vast differences in wealth across racial groups in the United States. The wealth gap between white and African-American families nearly tripled from $85,000 in 1984 to $236,500 in 2009. There are many causes, including years of home ownership, household income, unemployment, and education, but inheritance might be the most important.

Here's a straightforward question. For the sake of argument, let's assume that the average white family in the United States has $100. In those terms, how much money do you think a comparable black family has?

On second thought, it might be better not to guess.

Hardly anyone gets it right.

The correct answer is $5.

Think about that. This figure represents an existential crisis in America.

Most Americans guess upwards of $80. This is the crux of a new article appearing in the journal *Perspectives on Psychological Science*. Specifically, a team of psychologists led by Michael Kraus of Yale University examined the extent to which people underestimate the degree of racial economic inequality in the United States. Their results are alarming, to say the least.

Deep Dive

According to the 2018 State of Working America Wages report from the Economic Policy Institute, the wages for white workers grew much faster than wages for black and Hispanic (EPI's term) workers since the year 2000, and this was true from the lowest- to the highest-earning workers. Other findings from the report:

• At every level of the wage distribution, the gap between black and white wages was larger in 2018 than it was in 2000.

• Only black workers with college degrees earned higher wages in 2018 than they did in 2000, but their wage growth in that time was slower than that for white workers with college degrees.

• In 2000, median black wages were 79.2 percent of white wages. By 2018, they were 73.3 percent of white wages.

• White and Hispanic wage growth has grown four times faster than black wages, except at the very lowest and very highest levels of earners. That growth differential is not because of "some tremendous growth for white and Hispanic workers," but rather because "there has been little to no wage growth for black workers."

Challenge Questions:

Does any of this information change your perspective on racism?

Do you believe that institutional racism is an issue in the USA that needs to be rectified?

Did any of the statistics shock you?

What would the existentialist say about racism?

*Thank you to Wikipedia for some of the information and text in this article.

Deep Dive

THE RACIAL WEALTH GAP: ADDRESSING AMERICA'S MOST PRESSING EPIDEMIC —BRIAN THOMPSON

One troubling sign of the work we have to do can be seen in a wealth gap between black Americans and white Americans that persists and even seems to be widening. It's a sobering reminder of how far we are from true equality.

I have always known that this gap (or "chasm," as one author described it) existed, but I didn't realize how large it was until I started researching this piece. The facts and figures truly frightened me. Today, I hope to raise awareness of this problem and suggest some practical steps to help resolve the issue.

The wealth gap
The wealth gap measures the difference between the median

191

wealth of blacks versus the median wealth of whites. Almost all studies calculate wealth by adding up total assets (e.g., cash, retirement accounts, home, etc.) then subtracting liabilities (e.g., credit card debt, student loans, mortgage, etc.) The resulting figure is your net worth.

As I've argued before, net worth is probably the most important measure of overall financial health. It matters more than income, because high earnings, unfortunately, don't always translate into financial security. I experienced this often in representation of taxpayers before the IRS, several of whom had $300,000+ a year in income but over $500,000 of tax debt. While the income gap provides as huge hurdle to equality, the wealth gap presents a mountain.

Here are some of the statistics:

• According to the *New York Times,* for every $100 in white family wealth, black families hold just $5.04.

• The Economic Policy Institute found that more than one in four black households have zero or negative net worth, compared to less than one in ten white families without wealth.

• The Institute for Policy Studies recent report *The Road to Zero Wealth: How the Racial Divide is Hollowing Out the America's Middle Class* (RZW) showed that between 1983 and 2013, the wealth of the median black household declined 75 percent (from $6,800 to $1,700), and the median Latino household declined 50 percent (from $4,000 to $2,000). At the same time, wealth for the median white household increased

14 percent from $102,000 to $116,800.

You might think that the economic outlook for the black community and other people of color has improved lately, given our president touting black unemployment being as low as it's ever been. Yet RZW shows that far from getting better, the total economic picture for black people is still deteriorating.

Over the last two years, black and Latino households lost even more wealth: 18 percent for the former, 12 percent for the latter. After those declines, the median white household owns 86 times more wealth than its black counterpart, and 68 times more wealth than its Latino one.

If this trend continues, the median black household wealth will hit zero by 2053.

How did this happen?
The term "systemic racism" ruffles a lot of feathers. It often triggers emotional arguments about how people feel about racism and its effects. Yet concrete data over long periods of time shows very clearly that systemic racism exists.

Blacks were historically prevented from building wealth by slavery and Jim Crow Laws (laws that enforced segregation in the south until the Civil Rights act of 1964). Government policies including The Homestead Act, The Chinese Exclusion Act, and even the Social Security Act, were often designed to exclude people of color.

For example, in the 1930s, as part of the New Deal, the

Federal Housing Administration (FHA) created loan programs to help make home ownership accessible to more Americans. The Government created color-coded maps—green for good neighborhoods and red for bad neighborhoods—to determine who got those loans. Spoiler alert: many neighborhoods were designated as red because blacks and other people of color lived in them. This process, known as red-lining, systematically prevented them from not only getting home loans but also encouraged developers in green areas to explicitly discriminate against non-whites. This often led households of color into wealth-stripping "land contracts," where they paid exorbitant prices for homes that they could lose very easily.

These polices resulted in 98% of home loans going to white families, from 1934 to 1962. Not only did the ability to purchase homes give whites the ability to accrue wealth, it also attracted new businesses to those neighborhoods, which increased property values and allowed those homeowners access to other wealth building vehicles like going to college. As a result, wealth in the white communities compounded and passed to future generations.

Even after these policies were eliminated, the lack of wealth still prevented minorities from moving up to the green neighborhoods and kept the communities separated by race. Additionally, certain structures like a racially skewed criminal justice system and the tax code favoring the rich continue to contribute to this divide.

The compounding effects of these types of laws have led to the wealth chasm that now exists. Even now, these effects are felt

Deep Dive

between otherwise similar families of different races. According to the Economic Policy Institute, the typical black family with a graduate or professional degree lagged its white counterpart in wealth by more than $200,000.

What can we do?

Racial wealth inequality is a huge problem that not only affects communities of color but also will have a lasting impact on our country as a whole. Some 70% of our economic growth comes from consumer spending. As black and Latino households grow to become the majority of the population, their inability to spend due to the lack of wealth and paying down debt will slow economic growth. We owe it to ourselves and future generations to start correcting this problem now.

So what do we do about it? Here are a couple of solutions.

Spread the word

First and foremost, we need to spread the word. As pointed out in the *New York Times,* despite these staggering figures, we tend to forget or dismiss the research. Do your part to spread the word about this gap and help build the collective consciousness of the problem. Now is the time to be vigilant and understand we have a lot of work to do.

To keep yourself informed, I strongly encourage you to read the entire RZW study. The mind-blowing research helps put in to perspective the severity of the situation and how the racial divide will have a continuing negative impact on our economy.

Support policies to end discrimination and engender parity.

We got into this mess largely because government policies encouraged wealth building for white Americans to the detriment of black Americans and other communities of color. To fix it, we'll need policies that will help close the gap. RZW points out that no one initiative will do.

The response needs to be widespread, including a racial wealth divide audit, improved data collection, and tax reform. The study highlights many specific polices that we can institute and their individual impact. While we as individuals don't make policy, we elect the legislators who do. So we should use our collective voices to support and elect those people, especially people of color, that can put this type of policy reform in place.

Financial education
The wealth divide isn't due to individual behaviors. However, because of the wealth insecurity, it's more important than ever that households of color make smart decisions with their money. So we need to start stripping away the taboos around talking about money and promote education for issues that particularly affect people of color. That will involve making the financial industry more accessible to people of color and creating programs like the Dead Day Job Army that support their specific needs.

I hope this inspires you to take action now.

This article was reprinted by permission

Challenge Questions:

To what do you attribute the wealth gap?

Should the United States consider reparations for African Americans?

Do you think that Red-lining is a real thing that is still happening?

Brian Thompson

As both a tax attorney and a CERTIFIED FINANCIAL PLANNER™, I provide comprehensive financial planning to LGBTQ entrepreneurs who run mission-driven businesses. I hold a special place in my heart for small-business owners. I spent a decade defending them against the IRS as a tax attorney and have become one as a financial advisor. It's a position filled with hope and opportunity. It gives you the most flexibility to create the life that you want. I also understand the added stresses of running a business while being a person of color and a part of the LGBTQ community.

PART 4
GOD
RELIGION

PART 4
GOD / RELIGION

This section explores different religions and perceptions of God or Gods. It has several essays with different, but not comprehensive, views of what the authors' religion or spiritual life means to them. I hope that the different views help you in your exploration of what you choose to believe.

RELIGION
—DAN BEEMAN

According to Wikipedia, religion is a social-cultural system of designated behaviors and practices, morals, world views, texts, sanctified places, prophecies, ethics, or organizations that relates humanity to supernatural, transcendental, or spiritual elements. However, there is no scholarly consensus over what precisely constitutes a religion.

Different religions may or may not contain various elements ranging from the divine, sacred things, faith, a supernatural being or supernatural beings or "some sort of ultimacy and transcendence that will provide norms and power for the rest of life." Religious practices may include rituals, sermons, commemoration, or veneration (of deities and/or saints), sacrifices, festivals, feasts, trances, initiations, funerary services, matrimonial services, meditation, prayer, music, art, dance, public service, or other aspects of human culture. Religions

201

have sacred histories and narratives, which may be preserved in sacred scriptures, and symbols and holy places, that aim mostly to give a meaning to life. Religions may contain symbolic stories, which are sometimes said by followers to be true, that have the side purpose of explaining the origin of life, the universe, and other things. Traditionally, faith, in addition to reason, has been considered a source of religious beliefs.

There are an estimated 10,000 distinct religions worldwide. About 84% of the world's population is affiliated with Christianity, Islam, Hinduism, Buddhism, or some form of folk religion. The religiously unaffiliated demographic includes those who do not identify with any particular religion, atheists, and agnostics. While the religiously unaffiliated have grown globally, many of the religiously unaffiliated still have various religious beliefs.

This is a fascinating subject to me—the exploration of different religions. I come from a religious upbringing. My parents have great faith. "The church" has provided them with a support mechanism to get them through adversity.

I see the value of the church and religion and have experienced it personally through many lifelong friends. However, I also see the nuance and hypocrisy of man using religion for selfish purposes.

In the end, I see God and I see Love. I see them as One.

I recently listened to an audio book called *Sapiens: A Brief History of Humankind.* In it, Chapter 12 explores The Law of

Deep Dive

Religion.

It asks, "What motivates people to believe in God?"

Why are there so many different religions, if they all claim to have the right answers?

This reinforces my belief that everything is subjective. We all choose to believe what we want to believe.

To me, the pursuit of knowledge is the most important endeavor of our existence. Understanding the role of religion in our lives helps us understand why we do what we do because our actions are a result of our motivations. Our motivations often come from the fear of angering the Gods or desire to please the Gods. As we know, some existentialists were very religious (St. Augustine, St. Thomas Aquinas, Søren Kierkegaard), and others were atheists (Friedrich Nietzsche).

Existentialism does not take a position on religion. It is more concerned with the self.

Religion is largely regarded as divisive in nature because adherents use "the word of God," according to their perspectives to judge, persecute, and in some cases, murder others for their beliefs in a different God or religion. In fact, more Christians were killed by other Christians than all other religions combined in the 16th and 17th centuries.

At the same time, religion is also one of the great unifiers of people in history, alongside money and empires. It forces people to adhere to principles that are considered universal and "ordained" by our creator. Religions establish norms and value that they consider binding. This allows for the control of masses of people.

In order to unite people, religions must espouse a universal superhuman order that is true always, and they must be evangelical/missionary. The best-known religions are both, but not all are like that.

"Since all social order hierarchies are imagined, they are all also very fragile. They larger the society, the more fragile it is. The crucial role of religion is to give superhuman legitimacy to these fragile structures. Religions assert that our laws are not the result of human caprice but are ordained by an absolute and supreme authority...thereby ensuring social stability and legitimizing laws." —*Sapiens: A Brief History of Humankind*

Religious history and evolution
Animism is often referred to as a pre-religion. It is inclusive of all living things without raising or separating man from all other living things.

About 10,000 years ago, we had both agricultural and religious revolutions. They seem to have been concurrent. Why?

We turned plants and animals from equal members of a spiritual community (animism) into the property of mankind.

Gods (religion) gained importance because of the implied contract between man and God for the right to move man into a role of being responsible for the management of plants and animals.

Polytheism evolved around 3000 BC. Polytheism means the worship of many Gods and the belief that the world is controlled by many Gods. Humans could appeal to Gods with sacrifices to ensure bountiful crops and food. It saw religion as the relationship between Gods and humans.

Polytheism does not deny the existence of one supreme being.

However, this supreme being is devoid of interests and biases in the operation of Earth and its inhabitants. This God is otherwise uninterested in the day-to-day happenings of human beings.

Polytheists embrace the concept of fate. For example, some years we get less rain than others to enable the greater growth of more crops. Praying won't help change that. Lesser Gods have specific interests and thereby can be appealed to for specific desires (more rain).

Polytheism is inherently open-minded—When adherents conquered other lands, they did not try to convert them to their religions.

Monotheism began in the 14th century BC. These religions say that the supreme being has interests and biases. For example, God loves us and is interested in the amount of rainfall because that will result in more food for us. Or God will help our football team win.

Monotheists are far more fanatical and missionary than polytheistic religions.

Polytheism still exists in monotheism. For example, people pray to saints for specific needs (like rainfall).

Of the monotheist religions, Christianity was considered politically subversive because it insisted its way was the one and only religion and there was only one supreme being—their God.

Christians killed millions of other Christians because they supported a slightly different interpretation of Christ's divinity of compassion and love.

Catholics added more responsibilities to Christianity. To enter heaven, they had to attend church and do good deeds.

Protestants disagreed and felt this *quid pro quo* belittled God's greatness and love. They thought that entry to heaven based on good deeds artificially magnifies the Catholics' self-importance. Christianity says, "God exists." Therefore, how do I please God?

Buddhism, on the other hand, says, "Suffering exists." So, how do we escape it?

Buddhism started in the 6th century BC.

Buddhism says Natural Law is more important than God.

Law of Nature—The superhuman order governing the world is

Deep Dive

not of divine wills, biases, and whims of God or Gods, but of natural law—the laws of Gods are subject to the laws of nature.

Law of Buddhism—Suffering arises from craving. The only way to be fully liberated from suffering is to be fully liberated from craving. The only way to be liberated from craving is to train the mind to experience reality as it is—not what we think it should be or want it to be.

Buddhism says that people are inherently discontent. Suffering is not caused by ill fortune or divine whims, but by behavior patterns if the mind is dissatisfied and restless. Their solution is to understand things as they are, then there is no suffering.

Ideology as religion/worship of man
Natural law/humanist religions include Capitalism, Nazism, Communism, Liberalism, Nationalism, and Socialism.

Humanist Religions started in 1500 AD. They advocate that humans are the center of the world and all other species are meant to serve humans.

In America, Nationalists believe that we have a special role to play in history. We believe free market capitalism with open competition and the pursuit of self-interest are the best ways to create a prosperous society. We are liberal humanists who are endowed by our creator with certain unalienable rights.

Theist (mono and poly) religions focus on the worship of Gods.

Humanist religions worship humanity (Homo sapiens).

Social humanism says we have a unique and separate nature, which is fundamentally different from all other living things. It says that the supreme good is the good of all human beings.

OR

Every other living thing is for our benefit.

What?

Really?

Every other living thing is for our benefit.

This makes me sad.

Of course, man is going to say that the good of man is all that matters.

This means that man can do what he wants without consequences.

Because, in the end, following the natural path from mankind to the individual self, man then becomes hedonistic and only cares about self-gratification, regardless of consequences.

This a problem of ego. Hubris.

Challenge Questions:

If all we care about is our individual happiness, then what happens to all other life on Earth?

And what happens to Earth itself?

What is the most meaningful religion to you? Why?

Do you think humanism is a religion?

What would existentialism say about the arc of religious beliefs?

Deep Dive

PROBLEMS WITH ORGANIZED, MONOTHEISTIC RELIGIONS
—DAN BEEMAN

Our belief in God or Gods and attendant religious tenets such as the Ten Commandments also shape our perspective on the subject and origin of these things.

For example, Christianity overtly teaches that man is weak, vulnerable, made in God's image, and a sinner. Sins can be forgiven if we accept Jesus Christ as our savior.

Catholicism is also structurally bureaucratic and patriarchal. According to these teachings, only celibate men who can't have kids can be priests. The bureaucracy is evident in the retention of land and power by the church. These resources can't be bequeathed to heirs, who can't and don't exist because priests can't marry.

I subscribe to the theory that God is love, and God is present when love is present. There is no need to go through an ordained male figure to be with God.

The existence of man and Earth are both tangible and universally acknowledged.

However, God is not tangible since you can't see, feel, or touch God.

Atheists deny the existence of God. So, God is not universally acknowledged.

Nobody has any selfies with God….As far as I know!

Therefore, regardless of our belief in God, we will not attempt to prove or disprove the existence of God. We will only give our theory of God, from our perspective.

Proof of God is covered ad nauseam in many other studies and is a subject worthy of deeper theological analysis by experts in that field.

However, we do acknowledge the significant impact of God (or the human interpretation of "the word of God") on human behavior.

Think of how often we hear about an insane act committed by a person who justifies the violation based on their interpretation of what their religion told them to do or say.

"God wants me to…"

Remember, existentialists say that an individual has free will—the power of choice.

So, to the existentialist, God may want me to, but I choose to act or not to act. I am accountable.

Hypocrisy in literal Biblical interpretation

On her radio show, Dr. Laura said that, as an observant Orthodox Jew, homosexuality is an abomination according to Leviticus 18:22, and cannot be condoned under any circumstance. The following response is an open letter to Dr. Laura from a professor. It's funny, as well as quite informative:

Dear Dr. Laura:

Thank you for doing so much to educate people regarding God's Law. I have learned a great deal from your show and try to share that knowledge with as many people as I can. When someone tries to defend the homosexual lifestyle, for example, I simply remind them that Leviticus 18:22 clearly states it to be an abomination. End of debate.

I do need some advice from you, however, regarding some other elements of God's Laws and how to follow them.

1. Leviticus 25:44 states that I may possess slaves, both male and female, provided they are purchased from neighboring nations. A friend of mine claims that this applies to Mexicans, but not Canadians. Can you clarify? Why can't I own Canadians?

2. I would like to sell my daughter into slavery, as sanctioned in Exodus 21:7. In this day and age, what do you think would be a fair price for her?

3. I know that I am allowed no contact with a woman while she is in her period of menstrual uncleanliness —Lev.15: 19–24. The problem is, how do I tell? I have tried asking, but most women take offense. Should I smite them?

4. When I burn a bull on the altar as a sacrifice, I know it creates a pleasing odor for the Lord —Lev.1:9. The problem is my neighbors. They claim the odor is not pleasing to them.

5. I have a neighbor who insists on working on the Sabbath. Exodus 35:2 clearly states he should be put to death. Am I morally obligated to kill him myself or should I ask the police to do it?

6. A friend of mine feels that even though eating shellfish is an abomination, Lev. 11:10, it is a lesser abomination than homosexuality? I don't agree. Can you settle this? Are there "degrees" of abomination?

7. Lev. 21:20 states that I may not approach the altar of God if I have a defect in my sight. I have to admit that I wear reading glasses. Does my vision have to be 20/20 or is there some wiggle-room here?

8. Most of my male friends get their hair trimmed, including the hair around their temples, even though this is expressly forbidden by Lev. 19:27. How should they die?

9. I know from Lev. 11:6–8 that touching the skin of a dead pig makes me unclean, but may I still play football if I wear gloves?

10. My uncle has a farm. He violates Lev.19:19 by planting two different crops in the same field, as does his wife by wearing garments made of two different kinds of thread (cotton/polyester blend). He also tends to curse and blaspheme a lot. Is it really necessary that we go to all the trouble of getting the whole town together to stone them? Lev. 24:10–16. Couldn't we just burn them to death at a private family affair, like we do with people who sleep with their in-laws? (Lev. 20:14)

I know you have studied these things extensively and thus enjoy considerable expertise in such matters, so I'm confident you can help.

Thank you again for reminding us that God's word is eternal and unchanging.

Your adoring fan,

James M. Kauffman,
Ed.D. Professor Emeritus
Dept. Of Curriculum, Instruction, and Special Education
University of Virginia

***

One of my favorite jokes is, "How do you know that God has a sense of humor? Tell people about your plans for the future."

Deep Dive

HOW MY CATHOLIC FAITH IMPACTS MY LIFE
—STEPHEN MUSTARD

I was born and raised a Roman Catholic from infancy. My mom was Catholic but my dad was not. He later converted to Catholicism when I was older. My mom's parents were Catholic and so was the rest of her family, so that had a major impact on building my Christian foundation.

At an early age, I had a desire to become a priest and maintained that desire throughout grade school. I became an altar server and always loved being around the church. My mom worked at our Catholic grade school and also worked in the rectory at church as a bookkeeper. She did the church bulletin on the weekends, and my brother and I would always be responsible to fold them in preparation for Sunday Mass.

I decided to go to a high school seminary in another city to see if that was the vocation where God was calling me. I went there the four years of high school and one year of college before dropping out and returning to my hometown. God seemed to have other plans for me as my parents were divorcing and I felt the need to stay close to home. The irony of it all was that my oldest son became a Methodist minister, so the vocation remained in the family.

In school, we had religion classes and learned the basics of Christianity from a theological standpoint. I guess that knowledge supplemented what I learned in the "on the job training perspective" growing up and being influenced by my family. Love for God and family and others was stressed early on.

I guess all of the above gave me a deep desire to continue in my efforts to pray and communicate with God and at the same time serve others.

Jesus, when asked what were the two greatest commandments, answered in Mark 12:28-34 to love God with your whole heart, soul, mind, and to love your neighbor as yourself.

So the question is: How does a Christian try (and I say try because we all fail at this all the time but we are called to get back on track as quickly as possible) to do what Jesus has commanded us to do?

Well if we look at the "saints" who have gone before us and those who are living among us today, we observe and try to imitate their behavior. Daily prayer is paramount and serving others is our calling. We can serve in many ways but the motive behind our serving is key. As Bishop Barron has stated, " Love is not primarily a feeling or an instinct; rather, it is the act of willing the good of the other as other. It is radical self-gift, living for the sake of the other." This is a lofty but achievable goal with God's help and He will provide that if we ask. We can be His hands and feet and voice on Earth because He cannot do it without us. This is the calling of all Christians.

Let me further say that there will be many struggles along the way. God has said that and believe me, we all experience them. But the faith and hope of a Christian and the love of fellow Christians is what keeps us going, and we need to keep our eyes on the prize: eternal life. God has said He will never give us more than we can handle and that is certainly true in my life. Thus religion has had a tremendous influence on my life and how I try to live it.

Challenge Questions:

Were you born into the same faith you have now?

Have you explored your faith or other religions?

What makes you follow the religion you follow now?

Stephen Mustard is a husband, father, grandfather (of 17 grandchildren), great grandfather and Stephen Minister. He is a sports nut (former coach when their kids were little) and especially likes the OSU Buckeyes, Cleveland Browns, and Cincinnati Reds. He retired from the State of Ohio with 41 years of service in the workers' compensation area. He and his wife Cathy live in Canal Winchester, Ohio, and are the proud parents of five boys.

LOVE, GOD, AND INDIVIDUALISM
—DAN BEEMAN

Existentialism requires a focus on the individual.

Being in love requires trust and focus on the Other. Love of God requires faith and trust.

How are they connected? What if God is love?

Our organic nature is to be attuned to our individual needs.

We focus on ourselves with self-love through self-gratification.

It is represented on the lower levels of Maslow's Hierarchy of Needs.

In order to love someone else, first, we must have our physiological needs met and feel safe, then we can begin to

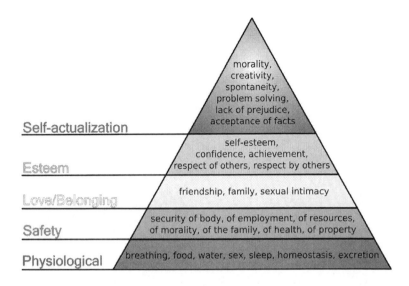

have an orientation outside of ourselves.

Eventually, with maturity, we realize that a life of self-gratification is unsatisfying. With safety as an anchor, we can explore that thing our parents gave us—that thing that brought us into the world—love.

The act of loving someone else and of lovemaking require the risk of opening ourselves to others. It risks the fear of rejection or failure.

It requires trust.

It requires a small step of faith that the other person feels the same, that you are emotionally ready to open, give yourself, and focus on the needs of the other in a tenuous power dynamic that also requires trust of each other.

Loving God requires a giant leap of faith?

Deep Dive

If our image of God is of some being outside ourselves, some all-seeing, all-knowing, all-powerful being that judges our every action, then our relationship with God is fear-based and inauthentic because we are motivated to be or act a certain way out of a desire to appease something outside ourselves.

"If I do this or act or think this bad way, I am going to hell."

"If I do this or act this good way, I am going to heaven."

In this case, the reward and punishment come from an external source. In this case, it does require a giant leap of faith.

However, if we can embrace the concept of God as a holy spirit or the love that exists within all things, then the leap of faith only requires us being loving beings.

Suddenly, there is no leap. Not even a step!

Love becomes an authentic expression of human nature, a product of love, living a loving existence.

I read this quote in an article and found it quite insightful and inspirational: "Real love is not to desire a person, but to truly desire their happiness—sometimes, even, at the expense of our own happiness. Real love is not to make another person a carbon copy of one's self. It is to expand our own capabilities of tolerance and caring, to actively seek another's well-being. All else is simply a charade of self-interest."

Note to self: Now it is time to live it. Each day. Love is an action verb. Step aside, ego, and let the love flow!

I wrote and shared this prayer one year with my family on Thanksgiving.

"Oh, Great God of the Universe. Creator, Giver of Life, Unconditional Forgiver, Abba, Yahweh, Krishna, Buddha, Jesus: You are not far away. You are present with us now. We are gathered here in Love: from Love, with Love, and celebrating Love for one another.

God is Love.

When we express Love to each other, God is present. God's gift to us is Love. God gave us children and partners in life so that we could more fully appreciate Love and God.

God gave my wife to me, and me to her, to learn from each other, grow together, and truly experience Love in its purest form.

You, my children, are an expression and physical manifestation of that love. Thank you, God, for blessing me with this love, for blessing me with you, so I can experience life, love, and God more fully. Amen."

Was I praying to an external supreme being or just trying to share that love with my family to help them understand how to tap into love as an authentic way of being?

Love in a family, more than just between two people, is possible but it expands the circle of trust and can be messy because it involves more dynamics and variables.

Now, expand the group to your extended family, your community, your village, city, state, country, and the entire human population. This adds many more variables, such as culture, education, ideologies, and paradigms. All are uniquely different.

Our challenge is that we exist on a planet with billions of other people who are organized into societies. Those societies are led by political parties or religions with different dogmatic or ideological perspectives.

There are two, opposing political ideologies: capitalism and communism.

There are problems with both.

Capitalism, unchecked, puts the priorities of the individual over that of his fellow citizens. It embraces competition, which pits people against each other.

Communism, in its purest form, puts the needs of others before the self. It says, "From one's ability, to others needs."

This ideal assumed human nature is giving and selfless. The assumption was wrong. It failed due to greed and corruption.

In a capitalistic society, the negative side-effect is the existence of an extreme divide between the "have and have-nots."

Those with wealth and power want to retain their wealth and power for themselves, because they "earned it." Those without wealth or power become resentful of those with wealth and power.

Neither trusts the other. Without trust, love cannot exist.

In a communist society, failure comes when people are not selfless. It fails when people pursue their individual needs at the expense of the rest of the society.

An example of this is the profusion of billionaire oligarchs who take advantage of the system to enrich themselves.

So, what is the answer?

The existentialists would say that we are all individually accountable for our own choices and actions.

I say, keep loving. Keep love in your heart.

Challenge Questions:

Where and what is God?

How do you communicate with God?

How do you express love to others?

How is trust expressed in your life?

How can you grow more love around you?

What is the best political ideology? Is it in harmony with others?

What would the existentialists say?

Mr. & Mrs. Beeman

Deep Dive

MY SPIRITUAL JOURNEY
—DICK BEEMAN
(A LETTER FROM THE FATHER OF DAN
BEEMAN AND SIX OTHER KIDS)

Dear Daniel,

I am engaged with your invitation to talk about the afterlife!

Our world's happenings nudge us to this consideration....

To begin, may I suggest that the essential encounter in the world is with the image of the Creator of the universe, the "Superior Power," Source Of Life, the Absolute.

The great spiritual and wisdom traditions of WoMankind have risen (and are arising) in our mutual seeking of ultimate meanings...our final truth!

These yearnings and collective stories across the ages, struggle with the profound truths concerning the human condition, and our access to the divine.

Every tribe, clan, and culture expresses unique but related symbols, narratives, and artifacts, morphing into religious gatherings, worship rituals, and practices of the spirit!

Perennial philosophy teaches that virtually every human culture evolved underlying agreements, seemingly with a basic framework: universal awareness that spirit exists, and that spirit is located in all traditions and works within and through all of us!

Dante's *Divine Comedy: Inferno, Purgatorio, Paradiso* (simply means a story that turns out well) is a classic entre' for the journey of the soul, "wiping the face with reeds...into the arms of Goodness."

Let's share our thought process and emerging beliefs on the path to eternity?

Ancient Biblical images project a striking view of what is waiting for those who "offend God": to burn in hell for all eternity.

In early church decrees, St. Athanasius declared, "Those who have done evil will go to eternal fire!"

Later, in 425 AD, St. Augustine warned of the "fallen state of humanity," based on the Old Testament, mythological story of the original virgin Eve, devilishly seducing the innocent Adam with a juicy apple...thus deliberately disobeying a judgmental God of the universe! The story goes that God imposed the "mark of sin" on Adam and Eve, and "fallen nature" on mankind...and to complete the narrative, necessitated the atonement sacrifice of Jesus, the God Man, to save us from our inherited sins!

So, an unredeemed humanity became corrupted by the so-called original sin of disobedience, which deserved condemnation by a faraway God!

Only the torture and crucifixion of the son of God could "save us from our sins"!

As recently as 1984, the Catechism of the Catholic Church affirmed the existence and punishment of hell fire and eternal separation from God for those in the state of mortal sin.

This overhanging theme of original sin and fallen nature begs for clarity and light...in our consideration of the path to eternity? Let's shine that light!

The pre-Socratic Pythagoras visualized "One with God."

"All will see God, start to finish."

He was open to new perspectives with his imagination and mental courage.

Greek tradition saw the unity of the cosmos as analogue to

the unity of numbers....(All numbers proceed from the number one, every other number continues to be its own self, as it maintains its unity with all other numbers and with its origin.)

Ancient Greek philosophy influenced Christian theology, offering the idea of "Creation as the Original Sacrament" (as opposed to "original sin").

One-hundred-fifty years before St. Augustine, Origen of Alexandra wrote in defense of universal salvation. He was called the "inventor of theology as a science." So there was parallel theologizing!

He proposed the story of Jesus the Christ as revealing the divination of mankind, rounding out the Christian economy! And the cosmic harmony between one and many!

Every intelligent being will see God. Redeem yourself by your faithful life process. Find unity with your Origen(!) start to finish. His Final Truth: "You are one with God!'

***

We all search and seek for how and what to believe, and what we are going to do about it!

I will tell you about my journey....

Jean Val Jean, in the wonderful *Les Miserables* musical, implored at the top of his lungs, "WHO AM I !?" That awakened me!

Did you ever notice the persona we present to each other is not

Deep Dive

the whole truth?

The ego-driven front I forward is not all that I am! (God knows.)

Husband, Father, Provider, Companion, and Business Executive, paid not by salary, but only by commission on sales of printing paper was my trademark identity.

My virtues were out front: proud of my popular accomplishments in the world! Aggressive, ultra-competitive, mentally toughened. Controlling, accomplishing external goals. Determined, winning the business battle!

Nearing retirement after 70 years, I retreated and wondered, "Who am I?"

My original counselor/companion, Sister JoGiaranti at the Institute Spiritual Leadership in Chicago, gently discerned with me, "Who else are you beneath your façade?" I joined a part-time community of religious mystics and lay ministers for three years of contemplative companionship, at the same time as my last three years in the business world.

It was an exciting, liminal period for me, of personal inventory, realizing my "false" self and shadow side. I was introduced to guided contemplative attitude exercises to transform core values and personal attitude.

On the street, I saw myself as "Heroic Provider." Is that all I had to contribute?

Little by little, over the past twenty-five years, I have been called to mentor and give spiritual companionship in the inner city of Chicago with the Cartegno family in Pilsen.

I have learned humility and compassion on my journey.

Grasping the sacred presence within offered a new gift of awareness and began my personal awakening and transformation.

Discover who you really are....Our process together!

Our deep yearning is to figure out our real self.

Spiritual development leans on self-awareness and change, at once and forever fathoming the experiences and insights of philosophers, historians, prophets, and universal theologians from every corner of the world, refining, reforming, clarifying the evolving energy field!

The Word of God made flesh.

This collective consciousness emerging may be seen as the grace of God, in process within.

On my journey, in my nature, I cherish this living grace...and welcome absolute mystery with radical, open-mindedness, imagination, and unfinishedness. I freely choose and receive the gift of Godness, and respond gratefully to that grace.

As a curious Christian, I choose and follow the life and story of Jesus of Nazareth, the God Man, the Alpha Person for all people for all time, believing in deep incarnation.

Gospel writer Disciple John, Chapters 1–14, quotes Jesus this way: "I am in the Father...The Father is in Me...and I am in you." This Bible poetry suggests the Holy Spirit within is our link to the mystery of the Holy Trinity...to be recognized and fulfilled!

The energy of our faith comes from a prayerful consciousness of our personal participation in the divine reality, our loving Creator God, source of all life and goodness.

We are called to receive, understand, and have the desire to express something sacred within us...to live out our true nature. John's Gospel says we are "saved" by God's transforming inner presence and our actions of compassion and love! (Together.)

My interests and personal evolution, on my path to eternity, have pointed to a contemplative attitude of simply seeking and practicing the presence of God in everyday life.

Sharing with you, I trust, will encourage our further conversation to unpack a dialogue of this intriguing mystery.

An active yoga practice is an instrument of contemplative attitude, which deepens the awareness of our, your, and my own, (and communal) fife in the spirit...which walks us on the path to the afterlife. This is how we are meant to be "saved."

Visualize the next life:

> "All shall be well
> All shall be well
> All matter of things shall be well."
>
> —Julian of Norwich
> thirteenth-century mystic

My love always,
Dad

Challenge Questions:

Can you guess where I got my sense of curiosity?

Is there one path to eternal salvation?

How does this essay move you?

Dick Beeman is a child of God. His journey has been exceptional. He found a true love through his devoted wife as a young man and stood with her in bringing up seven children. He spent a life in pursuit of epistemological knowledge and service to others, while supporting his family. He retired from business in his 70's to coach others in their pursuit of their greater selves. He is referred to by many as "coach" and serves as an inspiration through his daily actions.

Deep Dive

PART 5
EARTH

PART 5
EARTH

Our final section is about the planet Earth. What is your relationship with the planet that sustains you? I am currently living in Lake Tahoe, California. I am in awe of the beauty here. I can't imagine anyone wanting to live on another planet.

Our problem is that we think it can't speak for itself. It can. But it speaks a different language than we do. If we really look and listen, we can hear it screaming for survival.

Our planet reminds me of *The Giving Tree,* an American children's picture book written and illustrated by Shel Silverstein. First published in 1964 by Harper & Row, it has become one of Silverstein's best-known titles, and has been translated into numerous languages. According to Wikipedia, it follows the lives of an apple tree and a boy, who develop a relationship with one another. The tree is very "giving" and the boy evolves into a "taking" teenager, man, then elderly man.

Deep Dive

Despite the fact that the boy ages in the story, the tree addresses the boy as "Boy" his entire life.

In his childhood, the boy enjoys playing with the tree, climbing her trunk, swinging from her branches, carving "Me + T (Tree)" into the bark, and eating her apples. However, as the boy grows older, he spends less time with the tree and tends to visit her only when he wants material items at various stages of his life, or not coming to the tree alone (such as bringing a lady friend to the tree and carving "Me + Y.L." (her initials, often assumed to be an acronym for "young love") into the tree. In an effort to make the boy happy at each of these stages, the tree gives him parts of herself, which he can transform into material items, such as money (from her apples), a house (from her branches), and a boat (from her trunk). With every stage of giving, "The Tree was happy."

In the final pages, both the tree and the boy feel the sting of their respective "giving" and "taking" nature. When only a stump remains for the tree (including the carving "Me + T"), she is not happy, at least at that moment. The boy does return as a tired elderly man to meet the tree once more. She tells him she is sad because she cannot provide him shade, apples, or any materials like in the past. He ignores this (because his teeth are too weak for apples, and he is too old to swing on branches, and too tired to climb her trunk) and states that all he wants is "a quiet place to sit and rest," which the tree, who is just a stump, can provide. With this final stage of giving, "The Tree was happy." But, was the tree really happy or did a man write that to help humanity feel better about ourselves?

The author, vacationing sustainably!

Deep Dive

SUSTAINABLE TOURISM AND DEVELOPMENT: AN OXYMORON?
—DAN BEEMAN

sus·tain·a·bil·i·ty
The ability to be maintained at a certain rate or level.
"the sustainability of economic growth"
Avoidance of the depletion of natural resources in order to maintain an ecological balance.
"the pursuit of global environmental sustainability"

"We do not inherit Earth from our ancestors; we borrow it from our children."

—Native American Proverb

In the beginning of mankind, according to the Bible, there were two people: Adam and Eve. The story is well known about the temptation of the apple in the garden of Eden. This is a story widely accepted as factually correct and promulgated in Judeo-Christian religions. The story tells us many things, but one of central importance to this paper: Man is easily tempted and desires immediate gratification regardless of consequence. This character trait goes to the heart of success and failure of nation-states (communism vs. capitalism), religions, and the long-term likelihood of sustainability on this planet. The words in the Bible are words written by man about mankind (men and women)—how we fit into, or more relevant, rule over, the ecosystem and our role on the planet as guardians or masters.

It is a story we tell ourselves—that God created man to rule the world; therefore, we are not subject to rule of law and are above the food chain. Billions of people on this planet choose to believe it and live their lives in accordance with these Biblical teachings.

If true, asking mankind to change our behavior to reduce consumption, travel, and population is contrary to our organic orientation. We have seen no evidence that will refute that assertion. Individually, men can and do change, but asking mankind to change requires a fundamental shift that seems highly unlikely to occur as it is contrary to our nature.

So, if man is greedy and unlikely to change, and the planet is warming, and there are limited fossil fuel being consumed at a faster and faster rate by more people traveling to more places, more often; how can we hope for sustainability on this planet? How much less hope can we have for an industry literally fueled by massive oil consumption, which is a limited resource

Deep Dive

and erodes the ozone layer faster than any other chemical? Let's look at how this is related to tourism.

As the oldest and largest industry in the world, tourism plays a key role in the consumption of fossil fuels, global warming, and leadership in promoting environmentally conscious behaviors.

It can be a driver of change and an educator of ramifications of our collective behavior, if the industry embraces its role as a natural leader. It must accept the fact that human actions are the key drivers to using and diminishing non-renewable, natural resources that help fuel life on the planet. We must take appropriate action to mitigate our impact through fundamental behavioral change and technical innovation.

We are skeptical that, with a growing population, incremental behavior change will not be enough to change the arc of global warming.

In the big picture, it does not matter if ten billion people on a planet stop using plastic straws, if they are not changing their consumption and waste or managing population growth. While noble, proper, and important, reduction of consumption is not a panacea for the extended life of the planet.

We must be cognizant that the planet is billions of years old, human population on this planet is millions of years old, the first automobile is only a hundred years old, and the first plane that flew is less than that. The damage that mankind has done to the planet in the past hundred years is not sustainable.

We need to process information gathered from scientists about the human impact of global warming by humans, and on the human existence on this planet. There are also potential mitigating and mutable factors, such as the existing political leadership in the United States, who confuses weather change with climate change and deny the role of mankind in global warming.

We need to explore the existential question as to the true nature of mankind. Are we a selfish species concerned with our own immediate happiness or do we care enough to sacrifice short-term gratification to ensure that future generations can also enjoy the same resources and travel destinations as we do?

Unfortunately, that is the center of the debate: Human acceptance of our role in global warming and how we choose to deal with it or ignore it. If we ignore it, tourism will eventually be unsustainable because the natural resources will eventually be depleted.

If we choose to accept the conclusions of the scientific community, then we need to explore the history, context, terms, stakeholders, and the planet itself.

Sustainability in the hospitality industry means many things to many people. For years, and still ongoing, is the fundamental debate about what it actually means. There are many definitions and it is used by many developers as market positioning with true adherence to the ideals of being authentically sustainable.

In sustainable tourism, "Sustainability principles refer to

the environmental, economic, and sociocultural aspects of tourism development. A suitable balance must be established between these three dimensions to guarantee its long-term sustainability."

There are many human stakeholders in the tourism business: developers, communities, legislators, enforcement agencies, guests, and employees. There is also an unheard stakeholder: the planet. It can't speak with words, only through the ramifications of human behavior (consumption, abuse, etc.) and the attendant manifestations of our impact on it.

Each stakeholder has a unique and differing agenda with their perspective, which is often in conflict with the others.

The goal of sustainable tourism is noble and worthwhile. However, it only works in the tourism business when the sustainable practices help maximize net profit. It does not work when practicing sustainability costs the business and cuts into net profits.

Businesses view success through profit and loss statements, which have no line item for how well the asset is sustained on a micro or macro level.

The micro perspective is mostly concerned with the physical infrastructure and community versus a macro structure, which is more concerned with long-term, global issues like global warming and the by-product of it, like rising ocean levels, the bleaching of reefs, diversity in species reduction, and more.

If success in sustainable tourism is judged through the lens of business and profit, it will have conflicting agendas with success as a sustainable entity over time, unless the sustainable practices regenerate the actual environment on both micro and macro levels.

Success does not have an adequate, universal definition. In a capitalistic society, success is mostly defined in business terms like profit and loss, asset value, price per share, yield, and more. Outside of capitalism, success may be defined completely differently with happiness as a primary component of how it is measured.

This subjective definition of terms leads to semantic challenges. If anything is sustainable, it is either sustainable or not, regardless of time frame, unless those time parameters are defined in advance of measuring sustainability.

Therefore, sustainability must be either successfully sustainable forever or unsustainable, as defined by universal human authority.

Well, forever is a long time.

If man controls the environment, human consumption, population, and technology, and defines terms like success, sustainable tourism, and tourism, and concepts like capitalism and communism, then we must address the very nature of man and our assumed authority.

Fundamentally, are we selfish or unselfish beings? Can we be

Deep Dive

both?

Do we view the planet as a living thing? I can't imagine why not. All life forms are supported by the planet. It is the life source; therefore, it must be considered a living thing.

If human beings are fundamentally selfish, then we don't care about our impact on the planet or the ramifications of our behavior for future generations. Sustainable tourism cannot be successful because behavior will not change.

If we deny the existence of global warming and the human causes, sustainable tourism cannot exist because we are unwilling to change behaviors.

If sustainable tourism practices in a capitalistic society cost more than doing things in an unsustainable way, sustainable tourism cannot be successful because the business has no economic benefit. And businesses that lose money eventually fail and close.

Therefore, sustainable tourism can ONLY work if:

Mankind is not selfish, AND

we recognize the planet as a living thing, AND

businesses can be more profitable by employing sustainable tourism practices versus unsustainable ones, AND

new technologies are discovered and implemented to minimize

waste, efficiently convert natural energy, etc., AND

government legislates and enforces environmentally friendly laws, AND

investors look beyond P&L statements to humanistic returns, AND

people ethically choose to work with, and for, businesses based on their environmental footprint, AND

we acknowledge our role in global warming and are willing to change our behavior regardless of economic or experiential implications on our happiness or satisfaction.

Whew. That is a lot of AND'S! The odds seem small, but there is a chance for sustainable tourism, if, IF, all, ALL stakeholders agree on EVERYTHING listed above, and take ACTION to implement completely and immediately without exceptions.

So, you're saying we've got a chance?

Well, not in my subjective opinion. But we will all be dead by 2100 anyway.

Because, although humans may not be selfish, we are limited, flawed, and make mistakes.

Admitting our weakness and desire for consumption/ gratification, we must turn to technical innovation for real, meaningful results.

Our chance for sustainable tourism over millions of years does not exist because our planet, like us, has a life span. Inevitably, regardless of behavior change, eventually we and our planet will die.

The good news is that we have defense mechanisms that prevent our understanding of concepts that are too robust or ephemeral.

Many of us can't or won't process big, nuanced issues with long time-frames and many variables.

Many of us are also still in denial about the basic facts regarding global warming versus temperature change or the human impact on our environment.

Our only hope for long-term viability (another 1,000 years?) is if we choose to be optimistic for technological innovation—the development of new ways to reduce waste, increased use of renewable energy, and significant behavior change by humans—yet-to-be-developed ways for humans to live in harmony with each other and the planet.

Let's walk down the path of technical innovation as a savior of Earth. The more we innovate technologically, the more machines are made by man to artificially impact Earth. Making Earth less authentic and more artificial with each innovation, which leads to a benefit for mankind at the expense of the planet.

We drill for oil. Good for man. Bad for the planet.

We use liquid mercury in our thermometer. Good for man. Bad for the planet.

We mine quartz to build computer chips. Good for man. Bad for the planet.

Why bad for the planet? Because they are limited, non-renewable resources.

Until we collectively look beyond what is good for man in the short-term, we can't make the right decisions on how to live or answer the question—What are we doing here?

Deep Dive

Challenge Questions:

Is man responsible for global warming?

Is tourism able to be sustainable?

How can you make decisions in your life regarding how you travel?

What would the existentialists say?

GREATNESS/INTEGRITY AND PLANET EARTH
—DAN BEEMAN

Greatness
The quality of being great, distinguished, or eminent.

"The greatness of a man is not in how much wealth he acquires, but in his integrity and his ability to affect those around him positively."

—Bob Marley

What makes someone or something great?

To me, it starts with having core values and is followed by living with integrity. None of that matters if your word is not good and your actions are inconsistent with your words.

Great people care for all the creatures on Earth, give their time, talent, and treasury to make the world a better place now and

Deep Dive

for future generations. They treat all people with respect, and they respect our planet for being the source of all life.

If Earth is the source of life and all that sustains us, why do we treat it so poorly?

We created global warming. We pollute. We are addicted to fossil fuels that are literally killing our environment and planet.

Earth is estimated by scientists to be 4.5 billion years old. They also estimate that we will run out of fossil fuels in only 200 more years. We have only been consuming them since the inception of the industrial age, or about 100 years.

Fossil fuels are one of the principal causes of global warming. Fossil fuels are a non-renewable source of energy. They draw on finite resources that will eventually dwindle, becoming too expensive or too environmentally damaging to retrieve.

Because of the worldwide reliance, fossil fuels are extremely valuable and cause conflict among consumers. Countries fight for control of it. People deployed by their governments are literally killing each other over it.

In contrast, because renewable energy is infinite, it is sustainable and can be shared by all. It can be exported by the country that develops the technology that harnesses the power. It can be an economic driver and create millions of new jobs. It can lead to peace and harmony by nations that work together in using it.

We cannot continue to destroy our planet and simultaneously

pretend that we care for our kids or their kids. The options are binary and directly opposed to each other.

Do we want to be led by people and associate with people who ascribe to our same values?

Our president used vague terms like "huge" and "great" when talking of his plans and people he was appointing to cabinet-level positions.

These appointments helped shape policies. Let's take a deeper look at these choices.

He chose Rex Tillerson as his nominee for Secretary of State. Tillerson is the CEO of Exxon Mobil and has close ties to the Russian government. The President-elect called him a "great man." He is a multi-millionaire with a $500 billion oil deal pending with Vladimir Putin.

He chose former Texas Gov. Rick Perry as his nominee for Energy Secretary.

Perry proposed eliminating the Energy Department, which is responsible for the country's energy policies, during his unsuccessful bid for president in 2011. In a debate during his recent presidential run, Mr. Perry said that he doesn't think "the science is settled" on climate change, criticizing "the idea that we would put Americans' economy at jeopardy based on scientific theory that is not settled yet."

He chose Oklahoma Attorney General Scott Pruitt to head

the Environmental Protection Agency, which is charged with protecting the nation's air and water from big polluters. Pruitt is known for the many lawsuits he has filed against the very agency he is now supposed to lead, as well as orchestrating the Republican attack on the Clean Power Plan.

He chose Rep. Ryan Zinke to head the Department of the Interior. He would oversee 500 million acres of land concentrated in the west and manage 1.7 billion acres of ocean along the coast. He also would oversee the development of nearly a quarter of the United States' energy supplies. In the senate, he has a long record of votes against environmentalists on issues ranging from coal extraction to oil and gas drilling.

Let's not judge words but actions. Well, these actions are screaming: "Oil rules! Our environment doesn't matter as long as we are creating more jobs."

"Greatness" in this case can be the collective action of citizens to stand up for our planet. The stakes are as high as can be for all of us. Saving our environment is more significant than hot button issues like immigration reform, race relations, freedom of speech, and the economy. Those are all important issues. However, they assume a sustainable environment.

Do we allow the destruction of our planet led by these "great men," who are clearly compromised by their interest in and support from the oil lobby?

Is this the "greatness" we want?

Let's Make America Great, but in this case, let's understand what greatness is and the necessary actions and implications of how we achieve it. Let's do it with integrity and in harmony with others and with this great planet which sustains life.

Challenge Questions:

How do you define greatness?

What makes someone great?

What does EPA mean to you?

What would the existentialists say?

CAPITALISM IS DESTROYING THE EARTH. WE NEED A NEW HUMAN RIGHT FOR FUTURE GENERATIONS
—GEORGE MONBIOT

The children on climate strike are right: Their lives should not be sacrificed to satisfy our greed.

The young people taking to the streets for the climate strike are right: Their future is being stolen. The economy is an environmental pyramid scheme, dumping its liabilities on the young and the unborn. Its current growth depends on inter-generational theft.

At the heart of capitalism is a vast and scarcely examined assumption: You are entitled to as great a share of the world's resources as your money can buy. You can purchase as much land, as much atmospheric space, as many minerals, as much

Deep Dive

meat and fish as you can afford, regardless of who might be deprived. If you can pay for them, you can own entire mountain ranges and fertile plains. You can burn as much fuel as you like. Every pound or dollar secures a certain right over the world's natural wealth.

But why? What just principle equates the numbers in your bank account with a right to own the fabric of Earth? Most people I ask are completely stumped by this question. The standard justification goes back to John Locke's *Second Treatise of Government*, published in 1689. He claimed that you acquire a right to own natural wealth by mixing your labor with it: The fruit you pick, the minerals you dig, and the land you till become your exclusive property, because you put the work in.

This argument was developed by the jurist William Blackstone in the 18th century, whose books were immensely influential in England, America, and elsewhere. He contended that a man's right to "sole and despotic dominion" over land was established by the person who first occupied it, to produce food. This right could then be exchanged for money. This is the underlying rationale for the great pyramid scheme.

And it makes no sense.

For a start, it assumes a Year Zero. At this arbitrary point, a person could step on to a piece of land, mix their labor with it, and claim it as theirs. Locke used America as an example of the blank slate on which people could establish their rights. But the land (as Blackstone admitted) became a blank slate only through the extermination of those who lived there.

Not only could the colonist erase all prior rights, he could also erase all future rights. By mixing your labor with the land once, you and your descendants acquire the right to it in perpetuity, until you decide to sell it. You thereby prevent all future claimants from gaining natural wealth by the same means.

Worse still, according to Locke, "your" labor includes the labor of those who work for you. But why should the people who do the work not be the ones who acquire the rights? It's comprehensible only when you realize that by "man," Locke means not all humankind, but European men of property. Those who worked for them had no such rights. What this meant, in the late 17th century, was that large-scale land rights could be justified, under his system, only by the ownership of slaves. Inadvertently perhaps, Locke produced a charter for the human rights of slave holders.

Even if objections to this could somehow be dismissed, what is it about labor that magically turns anything it touches into private property? Why not establish your right to natural wealth by peeing on it? The arguments defending our economic system are flimsy and preposterous. Peel them away, and you see that the whole structure is founded on looting: looting from other people, looting from other nations, looting from other species, and looting from the future.

Yet, on the grounds of these absurdities, the rich arrogate to themselves the right to buy the natural wealth on which others depend. Locke cautioned that his justification works only if "there is enough, and as good, left in common for others." Today, whether you are talking about land, the atmosphere, living systems, rich mineral lodes, or most other forms of natural wealth, it is clear there is not "enough, and as good" left in common. Everything we take for ourselves we take from someone else.

You can tweak this system. You can seek to modify it. But you cannot make it just.

Think we should be at school? Today's climate strike is the biggest lesson of all.

So what should take its place? It seems to me that the founding principle of any just system is that those who are not yet alive will, when they are born, have the same rights as those who are alive today. At first sight, this doesn't seem to change anything: the first article of the Universal Declaration of Human Rights states that "all human beings are born free and equal in dignity and rights." But this statement is almost meaningless, because there is nothing in the declaration insisting that one generation cannot steal from the next. The missing article might look like this: "Every generation shall have an equal right to the enjoyment of natural wealth."

This principle is hard to dispute, but it seems to change everything. Immediately, it tells us that no renewable resource should be used beyond its rate of replenishment. No non-renewable resource should be used that cannot be fully recycled and reused. This leads inexorably toward two major shifts: a circular economy from which materials are never lost; and the end of fossil fuel combined.

But what of Earth itself? In this densely populated world, all land ownership necessarily precludes ownership by others. Article 17 of the Universal Declaration is self-contradictory. It says, "Everyone has the right to own property." But because it places no limit on the amount one person can possess, it ensures that everyone does not have this right. I would change it to this: "Everyone has the right to use property without infringing the rights of others to use property." The implication is that everyone born today would acquire an equal right of use or would need to be compensated for their exclusion. One way of implementing this is through major land taxes, paid into a sovereign wealth fund. It would alter and restrict the concept of ownership, and ensure that economies tended towards distribution, rather than concentration.

These simple suggestions raise a thousand questions. I don't have all the answers. But such issues should be the subject of lively conversations everywhere. Preventing environmental breakdown and systemic collapse means challenging our deepest and least-examined beliefs.

*Reprinted with permission.

George Joshua Richard Monbiot is a British writer known for his environmental and political activism. He writes a weekly column for *The Guardian,* and is the author of a number of books, including *Captive State: The Corporate Takeover of Britain* (2000), *Feral: Searching for Enchantment on the Frontiers of Rewilding* (2013) and *Out of the Wreckage: A New Politics in the Age of Crisis* (2017). He is the founder of The Land is Ours, a campaign for the right of access to the countryside and its resources in the United Kingdom.

Our Planet/Earth. Are we masters or guests?
—Dan Beeman

Modern humanistic religions say that human beings are "made in the image of God with a unique, special role and different from all other species."

One of the fundamental questions we must ask is:
Are we masters or guests on Earth?

How we answer the question dictates our behavior on Earth.

If we think we are the masters, what type of masters/managers are we? Oppressive autocrats serving only our gratification regardless of impact or ramifications or on the other extreme, laissez-faire.

Do we manage or rule Earth as an autocrat without considering

Deep Dive

our long-term impact or do we let Earth and the Gods make all the decisions and accept the impact on our lives?

MANAGEMENT STYLE SPECTRUM

Autocratic
Managers make all the decisions with no staff input.

Persuasive
Managers make decisions and persuade staff.

Consultative
Managers make final decisions; however, staff contribute to the decision-making process.

Participation
Managers and staff communicate to come to a decision.

Laissez-faire
Employees make all the decisions.

Challenge Questions:

Are we masters or servants?

What are you?

Deep Dive

I read this final essay online and was instantly moved by the writing and subject matter. I reached out to this woman who I had never met and asked her if she would like to be part of my book of essays on existential issues facing humanity. She read some of my work and agreed that I could use this. I am choosing to end this book with this essay because it is timely, relevant, challenging, and comprehensive.

Barometer of our Current Existence
—by Tash Pericic

There is no need to explain the gravity of the effect the Coronavirus is having on the world—we are bombarded with it day in and day out.

I live in Croatia, which has just closed all schools, restaurants, bars, and non-essential businesses for the next 30 days; we are self-isolating and practicing social distancing but a full lock-down, house-confinement scenario is probably on the horizon.

There is no sugar-coating the fact that these are scary times, but amidst the fear and uncertainty, I feel like I am waking up, like the world may be waking up with a fresh pair of eyes. The question that arose from within, as clear as the plane-free blue skies, is this:

What if the Coronavirus is the ultimate pause and reset button?

Deep Dive

As a society, we have been on a trajectory that is simply not sustainable. Perpetual economic growth is impossible, and GDP is a poor measure of a country's wellness. Mother Nature has been crying out for help to no avail. Our school systems are outdated. Our values are out of whack. We worship the wrong heroes. We are overly materialistic and have forgotten the simple pleasures, the things that matter most. We are connected but more disconnected than ever. Suicide and mental health issues are on the rise. We are creating only with the intent to monetize or go viral. We don't acknowledge our neighbors or the strife of fellow humans. We have forgotten how to plant food, how to properly nourish our bodies. We stopped moving for the joy of it but only in aim of getting the perfect "beach bod" or not moving at all.

In a world driven by progress, we have forgotten how to be still.

We avoid and distract because we don't know how to sit with discomfort and uncertainty. We have lost the art of conversation; we talk to be heard rather than hold space to listen and understand. We have energized our fears and ego rather than our inner guidance. We have taken our loved ones for granted. We chase money, thinking it will bring us happiness or we delay our happiness to some point in the future, "when I get *insert wish here,* I will be happy." We forgot we are part of a community (which includes nature).

And yet, a worldwide pandemic may just save us.

We wanted more time, and we have been praying for change; well, here it is—just not in the way we expected.

We are no longer looking to the stock market as an indicator of our society's wellness. Utilities, mortgages, bills, loans, and the likes are being suspended and evictions banned. Most governments are trying to find ways to protect their people, including small business owners. Health, safety, security, and mental wellness are taking precedent over profit for possibly the first time, ever. We have no choice but to question our spending habits. Will we finally see that money and the economy are volatile institutions to build a society upon or rest our happiness on?

From the safety of our homes, we watch as the air clears in China and as Venice's canals shimmer an emerald green. As humans have retreated, nature is flourishing. Mother nature is showing us that she can recover, when given the chance. Is it possible we emerge from our homes with a new understanding of our connection to and impact on the natural world? Will we be more willing to acknowledge and protect it, less likely to take it for granted?

Children are at home with their parents and siblings, maybe learning the school curriculum, having the chance to be kids or even to learn some useful life skills like baking and cleaning. Yesterday, I watched (from a distance) a mother hiking with her two young children, pointing out the names of plants to them—is this not learning? Universities are offering courses for free—could this not be the new norm? People in every field, from literature and the sciences to art and music are offering their skills, services, or courses for free—a new currency?

Isolated at home, I oddly feel more connected than ever. I have been consciously contacting friends and family daily and we are talking, really talking and listening. We talk of true and very real fears but still, the conversations cycle back to hope. During some of the darkest phases of my life, I never reached out to talk but now, it's as if knowing that everyone is going through the same thing, has inspired me to forget "self" and reach out. When this passes, we need to remember that no matter what we are going through, we are never alone—someone has been through it, someone is going through it, someone will stand by our side as we navigate it.

We are self-isolating to the financial detriment of ourselves but for the greater good of the community. Initiatives are springing up everywhere in the aim of helping our neighbors, the elderly, and vulnerable members of society. We can finally see who the true heroes are; not Insta-stars but instead scientists, doctors, nurses, teachers, bus drivers, people working in supermarkets.... All of the "unskilled workers" are the ones keeping our society functioning, putting their health on the line for the whole— these are the real heroes. People are standing at their windows, sending out rounds of applause to these unsung heroes.

Can we please remember this when the (new) normalcy returns?

I see empty shelves in the plant sections and think "yes," we are remembering that we can plant our own food and try to live more sustainably. We are choosing food that has actual nutritional value instead of processed crap. Confined to our homes, we are realizing we have taken movement for granted and are vowing never to do so again. Those of us who can are getting out in nature, appreciating it with a new pair of eyes, aware that it is a luxury that can be taken from us. Those who can't are finding new and creative ways to move at home that don't cost a thing!

We are creating for the sake of creating because it is what we were born to do. Not just to make money or become YouTube famous but because it's what is written on our hearts. How many books, poems, and paintings are going to be born during this time? We are all turning to the arts to keep us entertained and sane. Does this mean we can finally dismiss the notion that "there is no value in the arts"?

People are laughing, performing concerts from their living rooms and balconies, or hanging out of their windows to sing to their neighbors—even as I write this sentence, I smile. We are filling the darkness with so much light and joy that it makes me want to cry and has redeemed my faith in humanity.

With so much uncertainty we are finally realizing the truth—we have no control over the future (we never did), all we ever have is "now" and it is up to us what we do with it; happiness is a choice. We have remembered that we are not alone, that we are one big beautiful community and we are in this together.

Isolation is also forcing us to be still. We may not like the uncertainty and discomfort that arises, but if we can sit with it, lean into it, we may inch toward healing old wounds. If we breathe into the stillness, we may even rediscover our inner guidance, our intuition, that little voice that whispers from our heart and knows what our soul needs—the same voice we have tried to silence or ignore for too long. There is a space and need for this wisdom, will we listen?

Everything we are seeing right now is proof that in times of darkness, we can still find love, joy, and beauty if we look, and, if we can't find it, then we can be it.

Yes, there will always be the selfish and ignorant (people operating from fear), but I see more people shining a light in the dark and I have hope. Yes, there are people facing real-life stresses, particularly financial, but we are all in this together; it is not just one person, one country going through this, it is happening worldwide, so we will find solutions—we must.

The system may crash but isn't that what we wanted, isn't that what we called out for, isn't that what we need to create real change? The question isn't: "How are we going to survive this?" I have already seen how we are going to survive this—together. The real questions should be: "What are we going to do with this time, what are we going to learn from this, and how are we going to build a better future together?"

In nature, some trees need fire for their seeds to sprout; maybe we need everything we know to "burn" so we can start afresh.

I know it is going to get worse before it gets better, but I have hope. We will get through this, together. Stay safe, healthy, and sane. Be the light for someone else.

Remember to breathe. This too shall pass.

Pause. Reset.

Originally published on *Elephant Journal.*

Challenge Questions:

How has the global pandemic affected your life?

Do you think society can and will change as a result of the pandemic?

How are you living more consciously since the pandemic?

Deep Dive

SUMMARY
—BY DAN BEEMAN

What a dive! Let's do a decompression stop here before surfacing.

What am I doing here? You have heard from some very diverse voices and opinions. Each one is subjective according to their individual life experience on Earth. Hopefully, whether you agreed with them or not, you answered the questions the essays asked and that helped you dive deeper into your understanding of yourself.

The essays all had opinions and perspectives from human beings on topics related to the human experience on Earth— existentialism.

Existentialism is one philosophy about the human existence. Therefore, I chose to use this philosophy to apply knowledge from authors of books that influenced my life. The books

277

were not about existentialism but did have existential themes in the stories they told, whether it was accountability to a set of principles, religion, God, or themselves.

So, while diverse, there is a common thread in the words they all shared.

Here are some examples from authors of the influential books to reiterate my point.

"Every human has four endowments—self-awareness, conscience, independent will, and creative imagination. These give us the ultimate human freedom….The power to choose, to respond, to change."

—Stephen Covey

"You and I are essentially infinite choice-makers. In every moment of our existence, we are in that field of all possibilities where we have access to an infinity of choices."

—Deepak Chopra

"A man who becomes conscious of the responsibility he bears toward a human being who affectionately waits for him, or to an unfinished work, will never be able to throw away his life. He knows the 'why' for his existence and will be able to bear almost any 'how.'"

—Viktor E. Frank

What connects the essays you read and the authors of the books that served as the inspiration is a connection between self, humanity, Earth, and the Gods.

All essays are subjective and come from the perspective of the author. You don't have to agree with them. They are meant to help you dive deeper to explore how you feel on the issues.

Deep Dive

Conclusion / Epilogue
—By Dan Beeman

Hopefully, this deep dive allowed you to take some time away from your busy life to read, pause, reflect, and consider your role in the story of mankind. Your story—the one for yourself that no one else will see, or really know. The one that tells the truth. This exploration will help you find your truth. Your truth, in alignment with others, if honorable, will help ensure a future for mankind.

The work we did in this book began with understanding ourselves and existentialism, then we did some work on understanding ourselves. We identified our distractions and shortcomings. Then we processed the essays. Throughout the book, we had a series of exercises to help us dive deeper into understanding our passion, purpose, mission, goals, and paradigms. This brings us to the conclusion—how we apply deeper learning of ourselves to create more meaning in our lives. This is an ongoing, never-ending process. As we learned from *The Alchemist,* life is much more about the journey than the destination.

A Buddhist existentialist would focus on living in the present, while holding themselves accountable for their destiny.

A Christian existentialist would live according to Biblical teachings, while balancing personal accountability for their life with serving their God.

How you live your life depends on your perspective blended with your priorities and inspired by your passions.

This book is either the beginning or somewhere before the end of your story—your journey. It is not the end. The journey of introspection is never ending. Nor should it ever end, for we can all learn something every day. Every moment is a learning opportunity.

For me, this too is a journey. Or a deep dive. It is not where we end up that is important, but what we experience along the way—that is the joy of the journey.

This dive can be a metaphor for your life as it is mine: Never stop exploring!

Let's see what we accomplished:

What am I doing here?

You learned a bit about existentialism and the thought leaders of the philosophy.

You were able to look at all the distractions/impediments that distort your perception lens.

You were introduced to the inspirational authors, both their books and ideas.

You read and wrote authentic biographical documents.

You pondered the meaning of life for each individual.

You reflected on emotional intelligence and the gap between stimulus and response.

You did a deep dive into religion and the power of the interpretations of religion for mankind.

You thought about your definition of success and happiness.

You looked at your relationship with yourself, with others and with Mother Earth.

You explored your relationship with God and religion.

You explored your use of time, what quadrant you spend most of your time in, and how to manage your time according to your objectives.

You studied the role of mankind in the bigger story of existence on Earth. You explored the concept of sustainability: of mankind and Earth.

You learned about subject versus object orientation. You asked yourself how you view yourself and how others view you.

You considered hypocrisy, forms of government, and the true nature of mankind.

You thought about life and death and the people who impact your life.

You learned about the danger of ego if not balanced by humility.

You pondered the existence of guns in America and the second amendment.

You explored the racial gap in wealth in America.

You read about the delicate balance between capitalism, tourism, and sustainability.

You read about someone who nearly died and how that shaped the rest of her life.

You took a break, did some deep, slow breathing and absorbed the totality of this new information. You wrote professional and personal biographies.

You wrote a personal aspiration statement.

You diagrammed your perspective.

You wrote a personal mission statement.

You broke down your personal mission statement into specific categories with detailed goals.

You pondered your purpose and asked yourself:

What am I doing here?

"I'm starting with the man in the mirror
I'm asking him to change his ways
And no message could have been any clearer
If you want to make the world a better place
Take a look at yourself, and then make a change…"

—Glen Ballard & Siedah Garrett

***

This book was written to be a timeless, personal resource for you. It was broken into four sections to make it easier to read. It was intentionally not about "current events" but about existential issues relevant to people living in North America in the 21st century.

However, as of the writing of this book; we are currently in a global pandemic of epic proportions. In the U.S., it has closed thousands of businesses, unemployed millions of workers, caused billions of dollars of debt, and dramatically reduced in-person, social interaction.

Conclusion / Epilogue / Beeman   285

While I can't possible predict the outcome of the impact of Covid–19 on society, I can put a finger on the pulse of the moment.

How we respond to social restrictions and reduction of commerce will define the future of humankind.

We are faced with an epic Darwinian moral test:

Does our government enforce the restriction of human interaction and kill businesses to save lives?

Or does government disregard medical advice to protect businesses and the economy, while endangering lives?

How we respond as a human race will define us.

***

"The truth is that everything starts with a decision," said Simona Ksoll in the forward to this book.

In January 2020, I made a decision.

I decided to write a book of essays about issues that were on my mind. Even though I had never written a book before.

Even though I failed my entire Freshman year of high school English and then I failed summer school.

Then I got a tutor and finally passed.

Despite that and other deficiencies, I made a decision: to overcome adversity and manifest my destiny.

Deep Dive

As existentialists would say—be accountable to yourself for your actions.

So, what are you going to do?

Only you can decide if you want to apply the lessons in this book. Only you can decide if you wanted to do the exercises and answer the challenge questions.

No matter who you are now or what you have been, it should not have any influence on who you can be.

"What am I doing here" is solely your decision.

How you respond will define you.

It starts now....

Deep Dive

ACKNOWLEDGEMENTS
—DAN BEEMAN

Without the love between my parents—Sue and Dick Beeman—I would not exist, therefore this book would not exist. They served as an inspiration, mentors, guidance, counselors, coaches, and teachers. They parent with empathy and love. They constantly encouraged me to grow and learn. They created and nurtured this curious brain.

To my children, Callie and Cole, for always challenging me to be a better parent. I thank them for not consistently reading my e-mails and texts and for not allowing me to engage in their social media. This became the inspiration for this book.

To Simone Beeman for her empathy and never giving up on me as a family member.

To my cousin Sean Cleary for his deeply personal essays, always finding humor in life, for being my writing partner, for always having time for a call and always saying yes to my crazy requests.

To Chris Beeman for always checking in with me and being there for me, no matter what the problem or situation.

To all of my collaborators and friends who contributed to the making of this book. Especially Simona Ksoll, who wrote the forward and an essay. And especially to George Monbiot and Brian Thompson for allowing reprints of their articles.

To Paul Steinberg for living his life as fully as possible, opening his home to me while writing this book, and for dragging me up Rifle Peak my first week in Tahoe.

To Jason Bowman for allowing me to quote him and to learn from him through his writings.

To my SCORE mentors Elizabeth and Steven for their support and encouragement and helping me find my editor!

To all the people who questioned me/my actions or thoughts, I appreciate the inspiration for this book to chance to share my perspective.

To you, the reader, for using this material to journey inward, ponder the issues, identify your passion to find your purpose and live with meaning.

Dan Beeman in Tahoe

Deep Dive

BLANK PAGES FOR YOUR USE

PROFESSIONAL BIOGRAPHY

PERSONAL BIOGRAPHY

INDIVIDUAL ASPIRATION STATEMENT

PERSONAL MISSION STATEMENT

Deep Dive

Expanded Personal Mission Statement

Personal Goals in each category

Deep Dive

VENN DIAGRAM

Made in the USA
Columbia, SC
12 April 2021